KINGERLEE

KINGERLEE

JONATHAN BENINGTON

KINGERLEE
by Jonathan Benington

Published in 2006 by Larry Powell Management

ISBN 0 900903 53 0 (Hardback)

Designed by David Anderson
Printed by Nicholson & Bass Ltd, Belfast

CONTENTS

ACKNOWLEDGEMENTS

I WOULD like to thank the artist and his wife Mo for their generous hospitality during two trips to their home in Beara, as well as putting up with my persistent questions and commenting on my manuscript. Thanks are also due to Larry Powell for introducing me to the artist and his work and for uncovering so much information on the artist's early life; to Ed Forte who shared his memories of John's school years and joint visits to London; to John Minihan, Con Kelleher and Bryan Rutledge who supplied such superb photographs (additional shots by the author); to Rowan Hand for his expert interviewing skills and infectious enthusiasm; to Anthony Hepworth for his promotion, guidance and support; to Bishop Michael Jackson and Alannah Hopkin for paving the way with their perceptive published articles; to the many private collectors of the artist's work for kindly allowing their pictures to be viewed and reproduced; to Loretto Meagher, John Taylor, John P. Quinlan and Alan Barnes for mounting such comprehensive exhibitions; to John Good and Richard Moxley; and last but not least to my family for letting me burn the midnight oil for the last twelve months.

We would like to thank the following owners for their generosity in allowing their pictures to be reproduced:

Mr & Mrs F. Aherne, Ireland
Mr & Mrs F. Applebe, Ireland
Mr & Mrs C. Armstrong, Ireland
A. M. Collection, Ireland
The Baird Collection, Ireland
Mr & Mrs J. Ballance, Ireland
Mr & Mrs A. Barnes, USA
Mr & Mrs A. Bartell, Ireland
Mr & Mrs R. Berlin, USA
Mr & Mrs D. Boyle, Ireland
H. Boyle Collection, Ireland
The Byrne Collection, Ireland
B.P. Collection, Ireland
President William Jefferson Clinton and
Senator Hilary Rodman Clinton
Mr & Mrs M. Corboy, USA
Mr & Mrs M. Cronin, Ireland
The Daly Collection, Ireland
Patrick Donely, USA
Mr & Mrs D. Egan, Ireland
Mr & Mrs W. Gillies, USA
Celine Gonzalez, Ireland
Mrs M. Goodman, Ireland
Mr & Mrs D. Heard, USA
Rev. & Mrs Heberner, USA
Mr & Mrs J. Higgins, USA
Mr & Mrs M. Houlihan, Ireland
Mrs Mary Hursin, USA
Liadh Kelleher, Ireland
The Kearney Collection, Ireland
The Kelly Collection, Ireland
Nicky Kinsella, Ireland
Mr & Mrs J. Lancaster, USA

Dr & Mrs G. Lancourt, USA
Catherine Lyttle, Ireland
Mr & Mrs G. Matthews, Ireland
Paul Monaghan, Ireland
The Murphy Collection, Ireland
Mr & Mrs M. McAllister, Ireland
Mr & Mrs K. McBride, USA
Dolores McColl, USA
Dr & Mrs J. McGivern, Ireland
Mr & Mrs Hayden McIlroy, USA
Mr & Mrs S. McVeigh, Ireland
Mr E. Nolan, Ireland
Mr & Mrs M. Nolan, Ireland
Mr & Mrs F. Osborne, USA
Sir Anthony & Lady O'Reilly, Ireland
The O'Sullivan Collection, Ireland
Masoud Pourhabib, USA
Mr & Mrs L. Powell, Ireland
Charles P. Reagan, USA
The Rowan Collection, Ireland
Mr P. Shanahan, USA
Barbara Fitzgerald Sweetman, Ireland
Target Collection, UK
Emma & Sally Thomas, UK
Mr & Mrs V. Toner, Ireland
The Toner Collection, Ireland
Mr L. Walsh, Ireland
Mr & Mrs C. Watts, UK
Mr & Mrs K. Whealan, Ireland
Mr & Mrs B. White, USA
Mr & Mrs V. Wyer, Ireland
Samuel Zurawel, USA

INTRODUCTION

JOHN KINGERLEE has covered his tracks well. His geographical remoteness goes a long way towards explaining why it has taken forty years for his highly original and contemplative paintings to be unveiled to the world. To reach his home on the Beara Peninsula in West Cork requires a suspension of one's reliance on maps as accurate indicators of journey times. The fact that international flights now connect with Cork airport may further stimulate unrealistic expectations of the connecting road network. As it is, from Cork city a journey of two and a half hours by car, travelling in a westerly direction across Ireland, gradually unfolds. The roads are fairly straight and broad to begin with, but they narrow and twist and straighten again with increasing rapidity the closer one gets to Beara. Many would find the undulations disorientating were it not for the compensating factors of light traffic and scenery that can only be described as jaw-droppingly impressive.

On my first visit to the artist I arrived on a spring evening, the rocky shoreline basking in a lilypond calm that, seen from the elevated

road, functioned as an expansive mirror that doubled the image of every headland and fishing boat in crystalline perfection. For the last half hour of the journey the road became single track, rising, dipping and turning constantly until at last it reached a zenith, and then suddenly the panorama of Kenmare Bay was revealed in all its glory. A fall of snow earlier in the day made the tops of the distant Kerry mountains glisten in the last rays of the evening sun. It was not difficult to appreciate how such rugged, unspoilt beauty, such clean fresh air and clear vistas would provide an artist with unending inspiration. This feast for the eyes and ears (one quickly learned to respect the silence of the place) dispelled baser cravings – the facile appeals of our consumer society – without so much as a murmur of regret.

The artist's bungalow projects into a crook in the road, nestling beneath a hillside and facing directly out towards the Atlantic. The house is spotlessly clean. One leave's one's shoes at the door and is given mules to wear indoors, wellingtons to cross the lawn to reach the studio. Scores of paintings on board, canvas, paper and printed pages are everywhere, laid out carefully in rows and piles, all in varying states of completion. Finished paintings come into the house to dry above the kitchen range and on sheets of newspaper spread out in the bedrooms upstairs. I go to sleep with the intoxicating smell of oil paint in my nostrils, and on waking up am immediately compelled to throw the windows open and photograph the panoramic view of the peninsula, the bay and the encircling mountains of Dingle. Breakfast is homemade bread, toasted, with butter and homemade marmalade, and a mug of leaf tea taken with a teaspoon of honey from the hives in the garden.

The correlation between outdoors and indoors is as refreshing as the setting, making me realise with some horror the extent to which most of us are out of synch with our immediate surroundings. We have become birds of passage, and this is reflected in our global economy, sourcing goods wherever we can buy them most cheaply, irrespective of the human cost. But John and his wife Mo live an altogether healthier, more balanced existence. And the art I see everywhere around me is a key component of that philosophy. The pictures emanate the same light and colours I can see through the windows and on my walks. They do not describe the landscape in any literal sense, but somehow they pulse with the same energy, as if thrown up by the same natural processes that have shaped Beara into one of Europe's most beautiful wildernesses.

In years to come public perception will surely link Kingerlee's work as closely with this part of western Ireland as Matisse's pictures are associated with the Côte d'Azur and Monet's with his garden at Giverny.

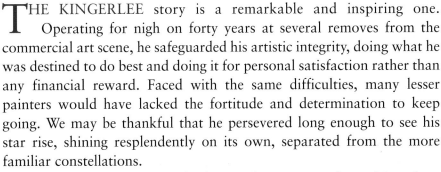

CHAPTER ONE

A PAINTER'S PROGRESS

THE KINGERLEE story is a remarkable and inspiring one. Operating for nigh on forty years at several removes from the commercial art scene, he safeguarded his artistic integrity, doing what he was destined to do best and doing it for personal satisfaction rather than any financial reward. Faced with the same difficulties, many lesser painters would have lacked the fortitude and determination to keep going. We may be thankful that he persevered long enough to see his star rise, shining resplendently on its own, separated from the more familiar constellations.

John Henry Kingerlee's background is very much working class. Born in Birmingham on 17 February 1936, he was the only child of Violet Mary Wedgwood and Jack Henry Kingerlee. His mother, who came from West Hartlepool and worked as a waitress, was descended on her father's side from the Hogans who came over from Ireland, and on her mother's side from the great eighteenth-century potter and industrialist Josiah Wedgwood. His father was local to Birmingham and worked at that time as a waiter. John's paternal grandfather had the reputation of being the strongest man in Birmingham. On one occasion he threw a docker out of a pub by clean-lifting him straight over his head.

The family left Birmingham when John was just six weeks old. They moved to Richmond on the outskirts of London. His father became the manager of a gentleman's poker club in Cromwell Road. With both parents working, the boy was looked after partly by his young "aunt" Anna Phillips in London, who broke and trained horses for the circus. A love of animals was ingrained in his psyche from a very early age. His earliest memory goes back to when, at the tender age of two, he was playing under the belly of a horse that was being trained for the circus. Despite being reckoned to have a dangerous streak, the horse was John's friend (it belonged to Tim Macleod, a music hall cowboy). Anna's boyfriend at the time was the noted film actor Douglas Fairbanks, Jr. (1909–2000), whom she met at John's father's poker club and who was spending the early months of the Second World War in London hospitals, taking special care of war refugees. The couple were so enamoured of John that they wanted to adopt him, but with the advent of the Blitz the Kingerlees moved to 32 Clifton Road in Paignton,

Devon, a faded Victorian bathing resort on the English Riviera. Thus was inaugurated the first of a series of westerly advances, a progression that would lead the artist forty years later to the very margins of Europe (whilst retaining a deep affection for the bright lights of London).

John attended primary and secondary schools in Paignton, but his pursuit of adventure took him beyond the classroom. While on a visit of a few weeks to a village near Bognor Regis, he got in trouble for picking up detonators, bullets and grenades from a Canadian ammunition dump and hiding them under his parents' bed in a suitcase. His father spotted him opening up a bullet and called the police, a response that must have seemed a little heavy-handed to the young boy. Safer hobbies included patronising any of the three cinemas in Paignton, where he indulged in the excitement of *King Kong*, the romance of India enshrined in the *Sabu* films of Alexander Korda, and the exotic appeal of the jungle as featured in the *Tarzan* movies starring Johnny Weismüller. He also had a passion for collecting American comics, which he scrounged from American servicemen in Paignton and on visits to stay with his Aunt Connie in Southend-on-Sea. His imagination was fired when he scanned the graphically expressed storylines in titles such as *Captain Marvel*, *Wonder Woman*, *Mandrake the Magician*, *Dick Tracey*, *Li'l Abner*, *Flash Gordon*, *Ibis the Invincible*, and *Bullet Man & Bullet Woman*.

Sadly, the words printed in the comics meant nothing to him since he was to remain illiterate until the age of eleven. It fell to his father to teach him how to read and write, school having failed to instil these basic skills in the boy. However, coming to this knowledge five or six years late only served to sharpen his enjoyment of the written word, and he embarked on a literary voyage of discovery that continues to preoccupy him to this day. He took to carrying a book with him everywhere he went, and sometimes his mother would have to drag him inside after nightfall when she found him engrossed in stories he was reading by lamplight. One of his favourites was *Kim* by Rudyard Kipling, which inspired in him an enduring love of India.

While John was given more freedom to roam than most children his age, exerting this right did bring him into conflict with authority figures on more than one occasion. Unfortunately, they generally responded by tackling the symptoms of his wildness rather than the causes. For example, he was thrown out of the scouts after letting off a firework behind the main tent, the scout leaders having falsely concluded that he was trying to burn the guy ropes. Incidents such as this led his parents to think that he was a 'problem' child, and the only way to cure the wildness in him would be to send him away to boarding school. Times were hard for the family: his father was out of work, he became ill suddenly and had to have a kidney removed. Perhaps the holy fathers would be able to instil in the lad a firmer grasp of discipline and obedience?

John's new home for the next six years was St Mary's College, Winslade Park, a Marist school in the village of Clyst St Mary, a few miles to the east of Exeter. The large house was originally built soon after 1782 by Edward Clifford MP, Sheriff of Devon, who had made his fortune in the East Indies. Upon changing use from a private home to a boys' boarding school it acquired an air of neglect and was unsympathetically extended, but with its basement, two storeys and attic it did not relinquish all its Georgian grandeur. The full-height, top-lit central hall was overlooked by two sets of galleries that contained the airy classrooms, whilst the extensive grounds took in playing fields, a large wood and a slow running river. Despite the strangeness of it all and the abrupt separation from his parents, John adjusted quite well. History, geography and literature were his favourite subjects. Sympathetic teachers included Father Murphy and Bernard McCabe, who were a great help to the rebellious youngster. One of his assignments was to prepare a talk on Exeter Cathedral, which dates mostly from the fourteenth century and boasts the longest unbroken Gothic vault in the world. During the course of his visits the building became a refuge for him, and he warmed to the sheer scale, magnificence and eventful history of this place of worship. Father Gartland was greatly pleased by his pupil's work.

Bernard McCabe, a lay teacher, welcomed John into his home and introduced him to the writings of James Joyce, Franz Kafka and Ezra Pound. This was a seminal moment in his education for it opened up a whole new world of culture to him, from the framed print by Paul Klee that hung on the teacher's wall to the books by Dante, Rimbaud and Verlaine that he was allowed to borrow. When he read Joyce's *Portrait of the Artist as a Young Man* he found he could identify with the sexual repression Stephen Daedulus experienced as a result of his Catholic upbringing. He took intense intellectual pleasure from discovering Joyce's wonderful use of language in *Finnegan's Wake* and Pound's in the *Cantos* – pieces of writing that feature amongst his top 'desert island' reads to this day. Other writers whose work he reads avidly include William Burroughs and John Cowper Powys.

John played rugby at school but was not into football. He enjoyed bird-watching and wandering in the woods. His rambles brought him into contact with gypsies, and he would visit their camp under the cover of darkness or at the week-end; he even learnt some Romany. Although the escapades involved a breach of regulations he managed not to get caught, thanks no doubt to being possessed of a self-confidence and maturity beyond his years. School life, however, got stricter as more pupils were admitted to St Mary's, and he only saw his family during the school holidays. As he got older his independent streak prompted him to hitch lifts on journeys that were too long to be done on foot, such as the 20-mile drive from Winslade Park to Paignton. He also hitched to Rome, where he was horrified to be refused a night's rest at the headquarters of the Marist fathers, even though they had over two hundred empty beds.

All boarding schools have their bullies, but John was well able to take care of himself in the rough house of the playground. He had several Italian friends at school, including the brothers Dominic and Ed

Forte and another boy called Italo, whose memory would inspire a series of drawings half a century later. While other boys of that era dreamt of becoming train drivers or soccer stars, John, ever the non-conformist, fantasised about becoming a bandit in Italy. This ambition stemmed from one of his boyhood heroes, Salvatore Juliano, who became a legend when he was murdered by the mafia because of an alleged sexual misdemeanour.

Creative activities during these formative years were confined mainly to the literary realm, with John being set the task of writing essays. His love of books led him to nurture another romantic aspiration, that of becoming a poet, but he also began to take an interest in the visual arts at this time. For one of his assignments he painted an imaginary bird (he called it an elephant bird), resplendent with the colours of the rainbow which were skilfully melded into one another. He would have liked to do more painting, but sadly he did not receive any encouragement from his family or teachers. At the age of 14 or 15 he encountered the work of Frank Lynch, a painter of beach scenes and bathers who lived in Paignton. Lynch loved to show his pictures to sympathetic observers and to talk about the craft of painting, and John proved himself an eager listener. Another artist he encountered at this time was Larry George, who painted on Brixham Harbour and applied his colours generously with a palette knife. The technique, by no means commonplace amongst landscape painters, would become one of the Kingerlee trademarks much later, during the 1990s.

On leaving school in 1955 John got his first job working at a bicycle factory in Aston. This was followed quite quickly by a return to Devon to help out in a school for maladjusted children. The school, which was at Kenbury near Exeter, was run by Esther and Fanny Kitto, a very 'alternative' couple who were constantly in trouble with the authorities. Fanny was a brilliant chess player who gave demonstrations where he would play a dozen or more people simultaneously. John's responsibilities were twofold: to run the grounds, and to learn gardening on the job. He got on very well with the school pupils and found, much to his delight, that he had a natural gift for making things grow.

Over the next ten years he would work in a wide variety of jobs, maintaining an involvement with the soil and young people whenever possible, and continuing to nurture his creative ambitions by writing stories and even a novel for children in his spare time.

A propensity for the literary medium is apparent from John's later habit of attaching poetic titles to many of his pictures, for example *Coming to the Man in Tree*, *The Heart is on the Wing*, *From Stone to Beast and back again*, *A Boat's in the Tree Day* and *If I was a Man I'd be knocking down my own Door* (the latter reflecting his instinctive disregard for physical barriers). Very few of his early writings have survived, but the existence of the following poem, penned after 1976, demonstrates that the writing did not stop completely once he made the decision to become an artist:

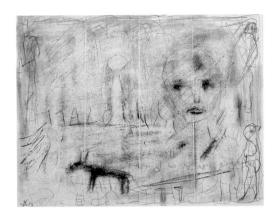

Italo Memory 4
2003, pencil on paper, 24 cms x 32 cms

And in the mountains
When I asked – are you afraid of dying
To my surprise –
He burst out laughing
In ninety-nine years
All living creatures shall be dead
Should all the world then be afraid he said
Is that not ridiculous?

Alone alone
Always alone
Lonely in childhood
Lonely in youth
Loneliness, loneliness down to the bone
And I wonder who put flowers
On my father's grave,
My mother asked if it was me
Now she too is gone
And there is none between
The grave and me.

After turning eighteen in February 1954, John knew that sooner or later he would have to face the prospect of being called up for national service. The Korean War of 1950–53 had brought an amendment to the National Service Act, lengthening the spell of duty from eighteen months to two years, with a further three and a half years in the reserves. Having had to share a dormitory with other boys for six years at boarding school, the thought of returning to a similar way of life in army barracks was not an appealing one. John decided to seek exemption on medical grounds, claiming that he had problems with bed wetting. He was duly summoned to an interview with the army psychiatrist, who happened to notice that the young man was carrying a copy of Kafka's *The Castle* in his back pocket, a book he knew very well. The conversation turned to literary matters, and it would seem that this unexpected discovery of common ground prompted the psychiatrist to be sympathetic towards John's case. In parallel with Kafka's story, this chance turn of events saved John from the fate meted out to land-surveyor K, the hero of *The Castle*, whose spiritual progress was barred by an impenetrable smokescreen of petty bureaucracy. John still had to go in front of a Kafka-esque jury, a panel of comfortably well-off, elderly gentlemen, but they decided to ratify the psychiatrist's recommendation that he should be exempted from service.

Deciding to make the most of his new-found freedom, he went off to London in search of fame and fortune, joining the Soho community of artistic and literary types. He arrived in 1957 and stayed for a year. One of his favourite haunts was The French pub, which, as he recalls, was frequented mainly by criminals and artists. Here he met Peter Everett, author of a series of novels as well as the book *Matisse's War*, a researched yet fictional account of the French painter's life during the

Second World War. He also met Quentin Crisp, whose autobiography *The Naked Civil Servant* brought him fame and notoriety for his biting wit and overt homosexuality. Crisp impressed John with his strength of character and his generosity, which manifested itself in his fondness for offering a meal to anyone who was hard up (a favour he did not extend to John, however, as he declared himself afraid of the young man).

One day the painter Lucian Freud came into the pub with two of his models. John was sitting on his own and could literally feel Freud's gaze from behind, burning into the back of his head. John is not overly keen on Freud's work, finding his representations of the human form neurotic, but decades later he would pay him a back-handed compliment by painting his own sequence of heads on top of the reproductions in a book of his etchings. Other colourful characters he met in Soho included 'King David' and 'Ironfoot Jack', the uncrowned King of Soho. The latter's name derived from his short leg elevated by an iron boot. He hung out at the French Café in Old Compton Street, popular with the bohemians, where he hawked his poems written on pieces of grubby paper and doubtless made an impression on the young Kingerlee due to his colourful way of dressing and talking (he referred to the younger woman who accompanied him as his 'Orniment').

In 1958 John married Maureen Riley (Mo), with whom he had been going out for the last three years following their meeting at Paignton Methodist Youth Club. The couple moved to Islington, John got a job on a building site and their first child, David was born later that year. The family would extend over the next six years to five children, with the births of Aram in 1960, Christopher in 1962, followed by the twins Ruth and Daniel in 1964. Besides being a full-time mother, from the very beginning Mo took a proactive approach towards supporting John in his career as an artist – a role she still performs now by organising many of the practical, day-to-day matters such as the mounting of drawings and collages, the packing of sold paintings, and the setting of the fire in the studio before John starts work. Her own creative skills have been harnessed not only in the garden and the kitchen using organic, generally home-grown or self-harvested ingredients, but also in the 1970s via the pottery she and John ran together out of their cottage in Cornwall. More recently, Mo's critical faculties are regularly called on to offer a second opinion on paintings that are nearing completion:

> " Mo's got a very sensitive colour sense, so often I will work on unfinished pictures that she likes, and they're always good. She's a much more civilised, sensitive person than me, in all respects, and I can learn no end from her. She sometimes picks the pictures out – that one's finished and that one's finished; and then I can stop working on those. "

At the beginning of their marriage, however, John had not yet made the decision to become a painter. A significant step in that direction was taken when he met the artist Martin Bradley, who impressed him by his

Self Portrait
frontispiece of Lucian Freud
book of etchings with paint-overs,
showing altered Freud self-portrait

Aram with Dog
1963, oil on board, 56 x 24 cms

resourcefulness in painting on pieces of wood salvaged from a building site when he could not afford canvas. John would sometimes baby-sit for Bradley in his house, and he remembers being very struck by the older man's paintings and the way he spoke of himself as a visual poet. The fact that Bradley applied his colours vigorously and generously and was working in a semi-abstract style indicates that John, even at this early date, was instinctively drawn to progressive methods in art (forming a corollary to his advanced tastes in literature). He painted a few watercolours at this time, not thinking anything of them, until an acquaintance whose opinion he respected saw some hanging on his wall and praised them extravagantly. No other encouragement, however, was forthcoming at this time.

Trying to support a young family in London on manual wages was beginning to prove well nigh impossible, so John and Mo decided to move back to the country and live as much as possible from the land. Through 1959–1960 they worked for the Camphill Village Trust at Botton Hall in Danbydale, situated on the scenic North Yorkshire Moors near Whitby. The Trust ran this 240-acre estate on the principles established by Rudolf Steiner, providing employment and self-esteem to a community of over 16-year old handicapped people. The ethos was driven by a commitment to working in harmony with nature, developing social and manual skills for the benefit of the individual as well as fellow residents. John taught gardening and farming. Lacking a car in such a remote spot, they were reliant on lifts to take them any distance greater then a few miles. Once John hitched a lift with a man who stopped the car at a telephone kiosk in order to enquire whether his passenger was "safe to be out", so taken aback was he by his fanatical behaviour. The incident can be put down to nothing more sinister than the fact that John is very passionate and uninhibited in his behaviour and speech which can sometimes be misinterpreted.

A more serious and potentially dangerous occurrence was the fire that broke out at the farmhouse where John, Mo and David were living. The cause was a burning coal that accidentally rolled out of the fire in the children's' bedroom upstairs. A fire engine attended the scene but was unable to get up the track because of the icy conditions, nor could the hose be connected to the mains as the house lacked a proper water supply. Although the building was razed to the ground mercifully nobody was hurt. The only possessions the family managed to save were a bundle of *Listener* magazines and some baby clothes.

Following the fire, the Camphill Village Trust found John a position at their branch in Newnham, a village sandwiched between the Forest of Dean to the west and a crook of the River Severn to the east. Here he looked after the cows and worked once again as a gardener, passing these skills on to young adults with learning disabilities. By the summer of 1960, however, he was back again in Yorkshire, managing an organic flour mill at Hunsingore near Wetherby. But it took more than a change of job and a new location to cure his restlessness. The following year saw the family moving to Hockley Heath in Warwickshire, 11 miles south-east of Birmingham, where they were surrounded by lush countryside that John felt was like the Heart of England. He worked in an organic market garden, used paint, ink and collage to make pictures (mostly of birds) in his spare time, and frequently attended performances of the Royal Shakespeare Company at nearby Stratford-upon-Avon, featuring stars such as John Gielgud, the young Judy Dench and Vanessa Redgrave. He found Shakespeare's use of the English language hugely inspiring, and to this day he remains awestruck by the creative outpouring that enabled the plays to be written in just under twenty years, disproving the notion that quality and quantity are mutually exclusive.

It was in 1962, whilst laid up for six weeks at Hockley Heath with a bad back, that John produced his first oil paintings, inspired by the view from his bed looking out towards snow-covered fields dotted with sheep. The results were unsophisticated but not without charm and atmosphere. At last it dawned on him that he had mistaken his true calling: he felt his natural path was to be a painter, the love of painting being far greater than the love of setting down words on paper. But for all that he felt at ease with the visual idiom, the couple of hours a day he had managed to dedicate to his art by rising early and painting before going out to work in the gardens were barely adequate. At this juncture he made the most momentous decision of his career: to give up regular paid work and take up painting full-time. His wife was behind him, and together they formed a plan that, while it was not going to sidestep the years of struggle that lay ahead, would at least make them more bearable. They would move to Cornwall in order to be near the sea again, and John would sign on the dole so they would be guaranteed some income pending any offers of exhibitions coming his way.

Sheep in Snow
1962, oil on board, 18 cms x 36 cms

With two young children to clothe and feed and a third baby on the way, and lacking any formal artistic training, this was an enormous leap of faith on the part of the twenty-six year old. After all, there was no guarantee that his art would bring him any more success than his writing or his gardening, but on the other hand he had nothing to loose. Despite their young age, the Kingerlees had already reached an understanding that there was more to life than the mere accumulation of material possessions. They would have heartily agreed with Wordsworth's assertion that, by "getting and spending, we lay waste our powers" ('The World is too much with us').

The paintings and drawings that survive from this period include landscapes, bird pictures, portraits of his two-year old son, Aram, and near abstract compositions such as *Meeting in the Forest* of 1961, a highly original work painted in a mixture of Indian ink and watercolour. It is evident that from the very beginning he made a virtue of technical experimentation. Furthermore, although his handling of materials has changed enormously in the interim, by 1962 his principal subjects had already emerged, and they would remain more or less constant preoccupations right up to the present day. But the twenty-year stint in Cornwall that followed brought only relative stability – the lure of London was still strong.

The following chapters, while not biographical in structure, use as their starting points the major themes of the artist's work, mentioning salient life events where appropriate.

CHAPTER TWO

ETHEREAL BEINGS

KINGERLEE IS an astute and dedicated observer of people. When travelling in the car or crossing a street, he will suddenly notice a face in passing and comment on its expression or physiognomy. On his yearly visits to Fez in Morocco he stays in an area where he is surrounded by small children, whose company he finds very stimulating due to their uninhibited joy, their craziness and infectious sense of fun. In conversation with strangers or acquaintances, he always seeks the person behind the mask, probing with his intellect, his wit and intuition as well as his gaze. He will tell a joke to a complete stranger (or strangers) just for the sheer pleasure of seeing and hearing how they react.

Other qualities that consistently come to the fore in conversation with Kingerlee include passion, freedom of thought and love of his fellow creatures. Preferring not to follow the herd, he is a natural questioner of the status quo and delights in finding things out for himself. Indeed, he regards the quest for knowledge – intellectual and spiritual – as a prerequisite for the development of noble character.

His life and career have to a large extent been defined by this thirst for knowledge, and he would be the first to admit that along the way he has taken more than a few wrong turns and blind allies. But one can learn from one's mistakes. It is surely no accident that one of the central themes in his work is that of the solitary figure, either in motion or stationery, heroically confronting his destiny.

In order to fully understand why Kingerlee continues to be so preoccupied with the human subject, no matter how abstracted and embedded in textured pigment it might be, one must look at his social and intellectual development. Is it possible that the different drummer we encounter in the art is paralleled by a similar attitude towards his personal development?

The boyhood encounter with gypsies proved to be a seminal one, for it was the first manifestation of a natural leaning towards marginalized societies, whose behaviour was governed more by instinctual triggers than by empirical information. In mid-1950s Soho, he made contact with another sub-culture in the form of characters from the criminal underworld. But he did not find his niche until he went to work with teenagers and adults with learning disabilities. This was an experience he found emotionally rewarding because of the residents' keenness to learn and the fact that they were not there under duress. He of all people could relate to this type of learning culture since his own

The Preacher Man
2003, oil on board, 15 cms x 10 cms

failure to acquire literacy skills at primary school had taught him the importance of cultivating a receptive mind.

Kingerlee's general reluctance to accept the given order of things, whether at an interpersonal or intellectual level, compels him to investigate other options. In the early 1960s he became very interested in the philosophy of Rudolf Steiner (1861–1925), the Austrian founder of the spiritual movement known as anthroposophy (i.e. 'knowledge produced by the higher self in man'). Steiner believed that the innate spiritual capacity of the individual had long been suppressed by an increasing devotion to materialism. The balance could be redressed through meditation and concentration, in other words through an exercise of the intellect that, theoretically at least, is innate in everyone. Steiner's conclusion that spiritual perception is independent of the senses had a profound impact on the budding artist, whose earliest surviving watercolours and collages (1961–2) were inspired by internal thoughts and feelings, rather than being representations of externally perceived objects.

Two collages of 1961 feature a stylised bird in flight above a circular pond with reeds growing to one side. These images, cut out of card, were super-imposed over a background painted in a mixture of Indian ink and watercolour. Another early painting (1962) showing a bird in a nest next to a line of hungry chicks was treated in a simplified style that owed much to the late works of Georges Braque, such as *Bird returning to its Nest* of 1956 (Pompidou Centre, Paris).

The frequent inclusion of animals in these early paintings inaugurated one of the dominant themes in his work, soon to be extended to include dogs, horses, donkeys, sheep, fish and mythical creatures, generally partnered with human protagonists. The artist's interest in animals stems from a deep-rooted sense of connection with them, coupled with an acceptance of the Islamic concept of Khalifa, or trusteeship, which requires us to preserve the integrity of God's creation – the earth as well as the flora and fauna in it. Kingerlee has worked with animals and lived alongside them for most of his adult life, and to this day he retains enormous affection and respect for "these other tribes of beings". The sentiment is underscored by a concern that mankind is endangering the survival of so many species.

The evocation of nature's presence that was captured in the bird paintings was transferred to several pictures including figures: one showing a Cubist-styled nomad wandering through a sun-drenched landscape guided by three birds (1961), and another with a scratched-out design of two heads in profile, male and female, who look at each other while a flying bird traverses the intervening space (1962). The very direct mark-making of the latter work has a primitive charm that contrasts with the sophistication of the earlier watercolour, but both seem to communicate the same message: that we are an intrinsic part of a much wider circle of life.

The move to Cornwall in 1962 may have been prompted by a desire to be close to the sea again, but John was also well aware of the county's popularity with progressive painters and sculptors, radiating out from St. Ives and Newlyn in the far west of the county, just as he

Heron, Warwickshire
1962, oil on board, 65 cms x 31 cms

Birds and Young
1963, oil on board, 26 cms x 50 cms

Lovers
1962, oil on board, 36 cms x 48 cms

took note of the area's rich Neolithic and Celtic artistic heritage. The need to find affordable accommodation in unspoilt surroundings brought the Kingerlees to Trevarrick near Gorran Haven, on the south Cornish coast some 35 miles to the east of St. Ives. It was in this isolated location, living a very hand-to-mouth existence, that John learned how to paint, teaching himself by a determined process of trial and error, innovation and experimentation.

Even at this early date he had already acquired a good knowledge of art, chiefly from books and magazines rather than visits to galleries. Inevitably he favoured the more progressive artistic styles, just as he did when it came to his other passions, literature and film. In the same way that he would solicit lifts from friends to see cult films such as *Pierre le Fou* and *Alpha Ville* in Plymouth, he hitched a ride to London in order to catch a show of work by Jean Dubuffet, champion of the Art Brut (Outsider Art) movement, at the Tate Gallery in 1966. Such a premeditated visit was, however, unusual, in that the artist generally prefers to come across art he likes in unexpected places, echoing the preferences of none other than Dubuffet himself: "Real art is always lurking where you don't expect it."

Gradually the Braque-inspired bird subjects of the early 1960s were phased out in favour of real or imagined figure compositions. *Is my Wife having Twins?*, an ink and wash drawing of 1964, shows his pregnant wife standing naked in a landscape, with a crescent moon and a large bird in the sky, while two silhouetted babies advance with their arms raised to greet her. The lyrical style of the work reinforces the positive message, which is one of fertility, portraying Mo essentially as a person at one with nature.

Other works from the mid-1960s show how he was beginning to move away from primitivised representations of objective reality. He made a series of meticulously worked pen and ink drawings that compressed countless heads and figures (up to 20 in one drawing) into a curvilinear design, reminiscent of Celtic or Gothic tracery. Facial features and bodily proportions were altered at will – again recalling the grotesqueries of Gothic carvers – in order to ensure that the overall design was not compromised. This type of free flowing gestation of the composition, putting an image down and allowing subsequent marks to respond to it, can also be compared with the paintings of the Danish artist Asger Jorn, a member of the Cobra group (1948–51). Kingerlee has long been a great admirer of Jorn's work, in which images are reduced to primal forms and interwoven within a unifying network of lines, tones and colours.

For materials John used anything he could get his hands on, applying acrylic colours to cardboard, canvas and driftwood, whilst the works on paper often incorporated collaged bits and pieces such as cuttings from magazines, photographs and technical illustrations. *Fairy Story: Death and the Goose* (1966) and *Horse Head* (1967) typified this new approach, in which elements of popular culture were removed from their original context and reassembled into the living forms of animals and people. This was probably the nearest Kingerlee ever got to a mainstream art movement, namely Pop art, recalling for example the mechanistic figures made by Eduardo Paolozzi and John McHale in the

Is my Wife having Twins?
1964, Indian ink on paper, 28 cms x 19 cms

Ibiza Drawing
1970, pen and ink on paper, 32 cms x 26 cms

late 1950s. The affinity with Pop, however, was only skin deep, a case perhaps of zeitgeist rather than direct influence. More far-reaching altogether was the inspiration he drew from the European tradition of collage-making handed down by the Cubists and by the German-born Dadaist, Kurt Schwitters (which will be discussed at greater length in chapter five).

In terms of content, Kingerlee's preoccupation with what might be described as magical or fantastic realism prompts comparison with the imaginative world of Paul Klee. The latter's tendency to turn painting into a form of creative play was something he could relate to, and indeed on one occasion he compared painting to a game, stating that it was the most enjoyable game he knew. In the catalogue of an exhibition from 1969 he explored the sources of his imagery: "My figures come from the subconscious – I don't choose them … They are not mythological." (Exhibition of paintings, drawings and collages, Foxhole School Exhibition Room, Dartington College).

The elimination of conscious thought from the creative process was of course nothing new, having been pioneered a generation earlier by the Surrealists. In Kingerlee's work, though, both during this period and later, the purpose was not one of uncovering hidden truths about the self, unleashing sexual fantasies or expressing one's neuroses. Instead, he aimed to use drawing and painting to turn the mind away from the material and physical facts of existence, thereby opening up access to a spiritual core, in much the same way as can be achieved by prayer, or the meditation and concentration advocated by Steiner. With the aim of facilitating this process the artist sometimes used drugs, namely hashish, and a sequence of pen and ink drawings that were made under its influence have survived from the year he spent in Ibiza, 1969–70. He now views the taking of drugs as damaging both to the body and the mind, having given them up completely nearly twenty years ago, but the drawings demonstrate nonetheless another facet of his seemingly tireless appetite for technical experimentation. One series was made by randomly dropping ink blots onto dampened paper so as to create an abstract image, which would then be worked over with a fine-nibbed pen, adding minute details of facial features, stick figures and imaginary creatures. If the overall configuration of blots happened to bear resemblance to a face, he would strengthen the shape and turn it into a head. Another group of drawings was more densely worked, depicting fantastic conglomerations of heads and figures in a variety of scales, recalling the Celtic artist's impulse to integrate every available surface into the overall design. It is not always clear which way these works are meant to be turned to be 'read' – something the artist himself seemed to acknowledge when he signed one of them twice, on the short side of the paper as well as the long side (this practice would be revived over thirty years later in some of his landscapes).

Other artists who have used drugs to coax images from the depths of the unconscious include the Belgian artist Henri Michaux, who made drawings under the influence of mescaline. In his book *Peintures et dessins* (Paris, 1946), Michaux issued the following statement, which could be applied equally to Kingerlee's drawings of the late 1960s:

Horse Head
1967, painted collage, 38 cms x 26 cms

Hash Drawing
1969, ink on paper, 10 cms x 16 cms

Mummy turns her Head
1969, Indian ink on paper, 43 cms x 27 cms

"You're drawing for no special reason, scribbling mechanically, and nearly always faces appear on the paper.

Leading an excessively facial life, we too are plunged into a perpetual fever of faces.

As soon as I pick up a pencil, a paintbrush, they come to me on the paper, one after the other, ten, fifteen, twenty. And wild ones for the most part. Are they me, all these faces? Are they other people? What depths have they come from?"

The 1970s proved to be a very difficult decade for Kingerlee. For two years following the return from Ibiza he was unable to paint because of a breakdown. The hiatus occurred at a critical stage in his career. Having had three solo shows in two years (1967–8) and been patronised by important collectors such as Ella Winters, Stanley Donen, Richard Harris and Leslie Caron, he should have been able to consolidate these early successes. But instead his work was in crisis. Eight years of sustained effort had not made a significant difference to his material circumstances. Reclusive by nature, he was not naturally possessed of the social skills that are required to promote oneself and one's work. He needed a champion, and although fellow painters Lionel Miskin at Mevagissey and Peter Liddle at Portholland were supportive and encouraging, they had their own livelihoods to worry about. Through Miskin he met the Jewish painter Patrick Hayman in Barnes – another self-taught artist with a passion for history, literature and the movies – and was so struck by his picture-poems that he adopted the formula in several later works (for example *Ah Sweeney Man*, 1987). Hayman's melancholic personality stemmed from his political and cultural displacement. He was the archetypical outsider, an artistic and social lone wolf in whom the younger man doubtless recognised elements of his own character. He was also a very good, and at that time largely undiscovered, painter.

Meanwhile, drugs and alcohol remained a temptation for Kingerlee, although he was beginning to realize that, far from aiding creativity, they impaired and stifled it. By 1972 the impasse he was in had waned sufficiently to allow him to return to the exhibition circuit and take part in a group show at the Prudhoe Gallery in London. But things still did not get any easier. In 1974, having decided a complete change of direction was necessary, he swapped pen and brush for the potter's wheel and clay. Perhaps ceramics would be easier to sell than paintings, given that their pricing reflected their perception as functional artefacts.

From 1974 until 1982 Kingerlee and his wife Mo ran a pottery from the front room of their cottage at Treveor. John used to take the finished, hand-moulded pots to London and set up a stall in one of the parks or squares. Prices ranged from £4.00 for a large candle-holder down to 35 pence for a finger bowl; even as late as 1982 his pendants sold for just 50 pence, each of them fashioned, netsuke-like, into a miniature figure or head, sometimes incorporating pools of molten coloured glass. However, the enterprise met with only moderate success. After covering overheads such as clay, transport, buying and running the kiln, there was little money left in the kitty. Meanwhile, he had a wife and five growing children to care for. On occasions the domestic pressures became too much for him and he would take himself off to London. In 1977 (ironically the Queen's Silver Jubilee year) he wound up in a squat at the back of Warren Street tube station. His straightened circumstances were a world apart from the salubrious setting for his fourth solo exhibition, Porchester Place in the West End, just a stone's throw from Hyde Park. Scrapbooks survive from this time with cuttings, scribbles, postcards and the odd drawing pasted into them, one such being a rare life study of a young woman seated, with her feet pulled up beneath her and her arms resting on her knees. The capital letter 'G' is the only clue to the sitter's identity.

Another drawing from the same year (collection Larry Powell) was executed on a diary page and is a masterpiece of minimalist mark-making, comprising two Cubist figures who appear to be running and holding hands at the same time. Their spontaneity is infectious, life-affirming even, leaving us in no doubt that the artist's quest for spiritual realisation was still continuing at this time. In fact, two pivotal experiences had taken him further along that road. The first occurred in 1969 when he interrupted his stay in Ibiza to pay his first visit to Morocco. Although he spent only a week in the north of the country he recalls that it seemed more like a year, and he still has vivid memories of the uninhibited zest for life of the people he encountered, which was so refreshing after the reserved behaviour he was used to in England. The second experience took place in 1975 at Bristol Gardens in Little Venice, when he made contact with the Sufis for the first time. Although it would be another thirteen years before he converted to Islam, he was struck nonetheless by the Sufis' strong family values, the constancy of their state of being, their cleanliness and their good character.

Now in his mid forties, he had grown disillusioned with British society, especially the drug culture that had taken hold amongst the young and the unemployed, and the uncaring attitude meted out to the elderly. A walking holiday on Ireland's Dingle peninsula in 1981, supplemented by a return visit the following Easter to paint with friends, were sufficient to convince him that he had discovered a saner and less spiritually bankrupt culture. Also underlying the move was the fact that "because some of my ancestors had come to Ireland and I'd had a Catholic education, I was always drawn to Ireland. When I got there I actually loved the place and the people. Then came a desire to come and live here and that's eventually what we did. A writer who lives on the other side of a mountain told us of a little house we could rent [at Cleanagh near Allihies, Beara peninsula], and so we came to the house and rented it."

The rent was just five pounds a week. John and Mo started their new life in Ireland in 1982, having left behind the pottery together with some furniture that a friend took into storage for them. They never went back for the furniture. Getting through the first winter at Cleanagh proved the toughest challenge, with Mo falling very ill with hepatitis. The only way John could raise the doctor was by setting off on foot and traversing the hill that separated them from the nearest house with a telephone. In fact, winters generally were gloomy, with four months

Scrapbook drawing
1977, felt pen on paper

Dancing With Joy
1977, charcoal on diary page, 12 cms x 18 cms

Untitled
1983–1986, oil on canvas, 50 cms x 30 cms

Head (Cleanagh)
1987, acrylic on canvas, 45 cms x 45 cms

when the sun's rays were unable to shine directly on the house due to the steeply rising ground at its back. Lacking a car and reliable public transport, the artist maintained this precarious existence for five years, balancing the hardships of extreme isolation against the extraordinary scenic beauty that was literally on their doorstep.

The cast of characters who animated Kingerlee's paintings did not change greatly following his arrival in Ireland. They still included pagan as well as religious figures – pilgrims, saints, the Christ child, Punch, magicians, wizards and their familiars. More prosaic individuals occasionally put in an appearance, such as a queue of five people and a dog waiting for a bus, and in the painting *Untitled* (1983–86) he even depicted a female nude. This picture was assembled from the same generalised, thinly painted shapes and forms that characterised other works of the period. The background is largely abstract, containing a cross and some calligraphic brushstrokes of a type he often juxtaposed with figurative imagery, thereby interrupting our reading of the illusion (he also used numbers and letters for the same purpose). The standing figure at the upper right of the composition has been roughed in with a few brushstrokes, just enough for the viewer to see that he is clothed, in contrast to the large striding female figure occupying the foreground, who displays her sex quite openly. There is a hint of the eroticism of Hindu sculpture here, and in one sense the picture can be seen as the female counterpart to *Lingam (Just the Whisper)*, which was painted in the same year. But Kingerlee's woman is not submissive or even particularly sensual: she retains a strong psychological and physical presence thanks to her erect posture and pallid, statuesque torso.

Around 1985 the artist added two large heads modelled in cement to the south-facing gable of his house, availing himself of the opportunity afforded by the re-tiling of his roof. The heads are not gargoyles, they do not serve any practical function, but one cannot help wondering whether they acquired, then or later, any symbolic significance, acting perhaps as household guardians or protectors of the harvest (the heads overlooked the kitchen garden). As relief sculptures with stylised features, they hark back to the figures and heads he was making out of clay in the late 1970s. On a technical level, being made from malleable material built up against a flat background, they also prefigured the multi-layered surfaces he would develop in the early 1990s using oil paint.

A painting of a head he was executing on canvas at this time was causing him problems. Rather than giving up on it, however, he decided to subject it to a highly risky and experimental course of action. He placed the painting outdoors where it would be at the mercy of the elements, to see if chance could resolve the difficulties facing him. Overnight the canvas was partially masticated by a cow, by no means a freak incident given that the cattle had been known to exhibit a fondness for cloth in the form of the washing. On discovering the chewed up canvas the next day, the artist felt that the cow's contribution, far from ruining the picture, had miraculously produced a perfectly satisfactory result. One corner of the composition was admittedly in tatters, but the fragmentary format seemed to be in sympathy with the dark, densely worked and rather Giacometti-like head. The painting was therefore saved by what can only be described as an act of God.

The majority of the pictures dating from the Cleanagh period were painted in acrylic. The move to Kilcatherine further up the coast in 1987 brought a rediscovery of the oil medium, which he could better afford now that his work was at last being exhibited (and sold) regularly in Dublin and Belfast. Still minded to keep costs down, however, he bought powdered pigment and mixed the amount he needed for each painting session with linseed oil. The shapes of heads and full-length figures could be etched into the warp and weft of the emergent surfaces, or summarily indicated with scrapes of the palette knife. The opportunities for progressively revealing and obscuring images were much greater than those afforded by acrylics. Using oils, he found that it was much easier to create ambiguous forms, relying on a greater degree of abstraction than hitherto.

This change was underpinned by Kingerlee's conversion to Islam in 1988 and the concomitant requirement that he should avoid direct transcriptions of the human form in his art. How he complied with this ban on making images – the purpose of which was to direct the mind of the artist away from objects of the real world – can be traced in paintings of the time. In *The Busker*, an acrylic of 1990, the spatial placement and definition of the figure have been denied by the broad calligraphic sweep of black paint that sits on the surface of the image, frustrating a three-dimensional reading. Another work of 1990, *Grey Bird Rider*, saw a switch to oil paint, and although the shapes of bird and rider were readily decipherable, they were creatures of the imagination rather than our own flesh and blood.

Coming to the Man in Tree, an oil of 1989, tapped into the same vein of mythic subject matter, albeit with a new blurring of the forms, as if to capture the movement of the two flying birds that dominate the composition. In *Twitter, twitter, twitter* of 1991 he returned to the human realm and, like the graffiti artists he admires, used simplified forms to denote the protagonists – an hourglass shape for a head and shoulders, and a peg-like shape supported on a stick leg for a full-length figure. An all-over scratchiness or doodling quality serves to heighten the tension between surface and image.

While the title of *Twitter, twitter, twitter* echoes the *Twittering Machine* of Paul Klee (Museum of Modern Art, New York), the subject matter was inspired by Beat writer William Burroughs' suggestion that "language is a virus from outer space." By virtue of being born into a verbal system of communication we effectively loose "the option of silence", for whether we like it or not, there is a non-stop monologue running inside our heads. In the painting, Kingerlee signals the dangers of gossip via the two yellow and black striped faces, which mimic the colour-coded warning given out by stinging insects such as wasps and bees. The implied message, therefore, is that we should try to regain the state of inner quietude enjoyed by nomadic peoples, amongst others, replacing words with silence, material concerns with spiritual aspirations.

Coming to the Man in Tree
1989, oil on canvas, 47 cms x 60 cms

Twitter, twitter, twitter
1991, oil on board, 30 cms x 46 cms

Three Figures and Bird
1994, oil on paper, 35 cms x 25 cms

A Boat's in the Tree Day
1996–2004, oil on canvas, 50 cms x 75 cms

The Local
2003, oil on board, 28 cms x 18 cms

Part of the fun of tracking Kingerlee's development stems from the realisation that it cannot be explained in terms of a straightforward linear progression. His use of imagery is a case in point, for even though the general progression since 1988 has been towards a greater abstraction, every so often he will produce a drawing or painting that bucks the trend. *Three Figures and Bird*, for example, dating from 1994, is dominated by a large head that stands out very clearly thanks to its treatment as a profile view, in contrast to the artist's habitual use of frontal orientation. The central figure's Easter Island-like countenance is framed on the left by a cloaked pilgrim (commonly seen in other paintings of this period), while a smaller figure stands to the right and is the only one of the three who is portrayed full-face. A bird hovers just behind the shoulder of the main figure. Despite the close proximity and contrasting scale of the three characters, it is still tempting to look for a narrative reading of the picture. Could it be a scene witnessed in a Moroccan market or street? Or is it a work with symbolic meaning, for example The Three Ages of Man? There is no one right answer, for Kingerlee subscribes fully to Patrick Hayman's assertion that "paintings are ambiguous creations which may have many meanings."

From the mid-1990s to the present day, the artist has consistently produced paintings of heads that are placed against neutral backgrounds, staring straight out of the picture towards the viewer. Most of these heads are depicted in isolation, but occasionally they will be lined up with one or two others as in an identity parade, or combined with full-length figures as seen in *Crazy Day, Portmagee* (2002) and *A Boat's in the Tree Day* (2004). The densely built-up surfaces of these paintings ensure that the facial features are treated in a very generalised, non-specific manner. The protagonists are ageless, timeless, garment-less, of indeterminate creed and race, sometimes sexless, although their paucity of hair generally gives them away as male. Lacking any profession or narrative content, they speak to us through the use of colour and facial expression alone, distancing themselves from the mythic associations of his earlier works.

For the most part the titles given to the pictures of individual heads (*Head I*, *Head II* and so forth) do nothing to remove the veil of anonymity that surrounds them. The only hint of any specific terms of reference was confined to a small group of figures wearing hats, such as *Sad Story* of 1997 and *Cloth Cap and Smile* of 1999 (Taylor Gallery catalogue, Belfast, 2003, no.37 and Leinster Gallery catalogue, Dublin, 1999, no.12 respectively). But even here, one cannot be sure whether the inspiration came from the movies or from real life. Then again, perhaps the hat was merely a shape that he liked to paint, as a fitting complement to the shape of the face.

In a recent statement the artist recognises the significance of the head both as receiver and transmitter of information: "my heads have landscapes and figures in them ... I see the whole journey of my life within the surface of these works." The reference to surface here is significant, for it implies a reverential attitude towards his subjects, a recognition that the paint he is pushing around is attempting to convey an ineffable reality, the sacred spark of life that unites us with our fellow creatures: "the human should turn to the light, be light, try and achieve the light." The sense of an inner radiance is notably present in some of the recent heads where the face, instead of being defined in darker tones, is conjured largely from smears and scumbles of white paint against a grey background. The ethereal nature of the resultant forms is a rebuttal of the importance our culture places on outward appearances, on physical and cosmetic beauty, challenging us instead to look beyond the shell and cultivate the inner self. This insistence on 'what lies beneath' has a cultural parallel in the beliefs of the Celts, who saw the head as the seat of the soul and an emblem of fertility, divinity and prophetic knowledge.

The artist's obsession with heads viewed 'full face' (rather than in profile) rivals that of twentieth-century artists such as Giacometti and Dubuffet. Both have certainly influenced him, but similar interests do not necessarily betoken a shared purpose: he lacks the existentialist take of the former as well as the crude, *faux-naïf* style of the latter. In 1995, with technical help from fellow artist Gerard Bellaart, he made a suite of prints of heroic heads and figures as a tribute to the Belgian painter of fishermen and peasants, Constant Permeke. He also finds ongoing inspiration in the fragmented physiognomies of Cubist portraits and the child-like treatment of proportions in the figures of Paul Klee.

But the closest art historical precedent for Kingerlee's heads is arguably found in Georges Rouault's numerous paintings of Christ. At the hands of the French painter, Christ is depicted as a Man of Sorrows, an indictment and reminder of the hurt and suffering that is in the world. While Kingerlee's heads likewise acknowledge the dark side of human nature, they differ from Rouault's by retaining the ability to see beyond the pain and the anguish. This quality is perhaps most apparent in a series of paintings entitled *Heads and Fields*, in which the composition is divided vertically by the dark trunk and branches of a tree, with a white or grey field to the left, and a red or occasionally yellow field to the right. The heads superimposed on the abstract fields are imbued with a remarkable serenity, sometimes even appearing to have their eyes closed, as in *Heads and Fields IV* (p. 127). The expansive foreheads and tapering chins of these heads serve to instil a sense of inner peace, as if they have arrived at a reconciliation of the two contrasting worlds embodied by the split image – interior and exterior, the self and reality.

Three Heads (detail)
2002, oil on canvas, 30 cms x 50 cms

Tribute to Permeke
1995, monotype with mixed media on paper,
30 cms x 19 cms

Heads and Fields II
2003, oil on canvas, 40 cms x 58 cms

CHAPTER THREE

REINVENTING LANDSCAPE

T HE SCENE that confronts John Kingerlee through his studio window every day is not a conventional one. His world is far removed from the landscape painter's stock in trade of fields, hedgerows, trees, farmhouses and winding lanes, receding towards a distant horizon. The phrase "between a rock and a hard place" would more accurately evoke Kingerlee's environs, although such a clichéd description probably over-stresses the bleak at the expense of the scenically grand.

Picture a foreground of rough fields divided by stone walls (as opposed to hedges), covered by grass that is good only for rough grazing. Trees do not grow here: the soil is too thin and exposed to the driving winds that come in off the sea. Instead, rock is everywhere, penetrating the turf in a series of imposing shelves, walls and steps that lead down towards the shore.

The middle ground of this scene looks reasonably tidy from a distance, just white foam breaking on black rocks that stretch out like skeletal fingers into the sea. Closer inspection, however, proves the unreliability of first impressions. The rock is actually formed into substantial corrugations that rise and dip steeply, eroded on the landward side by the wind and penetrated on the seaward side by fissures and tunnels. Only the cattle seem to be able to make sense of this three-dimensional crazy paving. It is all too easy to find one's progress suddenly and unexpectedly blocked by a deep creek or an unassailable buttress of rock.

The vistas that open up between and through the sandstone undulations bring a different tempo again, for the background of our 'picture' is occupied by Kenmare Bay, the body of water separating the Beara Peninsula from the mountains of Kerry. The visual presence of the ribbon of land on the other side of the bay is never a given, however, for the mountains are often veiled or else hidden completely from view by the weather systems coming in off the Atlantic. The sky changes constantly, complementing the movement of the waves and altering the character of the light falling on water, rocks and land. Because nothing remains static the photograph lies, or at best tells only a partial truth, likewise the painting that would seek to freeze a section of this panorama and contain it within a rectangular frame.

The special character of this south-western corner of Ireland stems from a realisation that here we experience Nature as a performance. The drama unfolds endlessly and is never repeated. It would take, surely, a very special kind of art to celebrate such an unconventional and yet breathtakingly beautiful landscape. Such an art would be born out of a struggle to survive in difficult circumstances. At the same time another struggle, a painterly one, would manifest itself, demanding years of dedicated technical and stylistic experimentation before reaching its definitive form.

Kingerlee did not settle in Beara in 1982 as an escape from civilisation. For most of his adult life he has chosen to live in remote places, far from the madding crowds of cities, towns and urban sprawls. Although he is no stranger to the quickened pulse and the confined spaces of city life, and indeed welcomes this experience as a periodic antidote to what is a fairly solitary existence, he is possessed of a natural tendency to gravitate towards the margins of civilisation. The two cottages that became his homes in South Cornwall (at Trevarrick, 1962–65 and nearby Treveor, 1965–82) are well off the beaten track even by today's standards, let alone those of forty years ago. Each is approached via a single-track road and there are no immediate neighbours other than the farm at Treveor. Though lacking sea views, these houses shared the advantage of being only a mile or so from the coast (Porthluney Cove being the nearest beach), with sheltered valleys and rolling hills in-between.

During the 1960s he executed a few seascapes with stylised fishing boats pulling in their nets, which would provide him ten years later with the basis for his little signature glyph of a man paddling a canoe. Several seascapes also survive from 1979–80, boldly executed with the aid of the palette knife in contrasting cream-coloured and earthen tones. But these examples are exceptions, for on the whole Kingerlee did not paint many landscapes in Cornwall. By not engaging fully with nature as a subject he may have been reacting against what others would have seen as an obvious career path. There can be no doubt that he appreciated and absorbed the scenic beauty around him, allowing it to seep into his consciousness, whence it would be resurrected later when he had more inclination to develop a personal landscape idiom. Suffice it to say that the scenery glimpsed through his windows and on his walks in this part of Cornwall was so unsullied that it could only have served to strengthen his feelings of homage and respect towards the land.

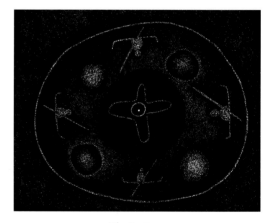

The Boatman
1972, pen and ink on paper, 26 cms x 31 cms

During the 1970s, Kingerlee channelled most of his creative energies into figurative work: drawings and paintings, together with mythical creatures modelled out of clay and fired in the pottery he set up in 1975 (there are affinities with some of the ceramics and bronzes of Asger Jorn). The process of kneading and working clay was an interaction with the very stuff of the land, as was gardening, that other activity which is so close to Kingerlee's heart. A large part of his enjoyment of potting stemmed from the fact that it put him in contact with the power of earth, air, fire and water, and he has always taken great delight in technical experimentation and improvisation. He would also have derived inspiration from the distinguished history in this part of England of making pots. Just a few miles away at St Austell were the famous china clay pits with their adjacent heaps of discarded diggings, whilst Dartington and St Ives had been bases for such famous twentieth-century potters as Bernard and David Leach. Indeed, the latter was so struck by the landscape of rolling hills around Dartington that he felt their strongly moulded shapes were analogous to those created by the potter's touch. The situation of Treveor, tucked away behind gently folding valleys and just a stone's throw from the well laid out gardens of Caerhays Castle (built by John Nash in 1807), is not dissimilar to that of Dartington with its medieval Hall and estate.

The Kingerlees' move to the south-west corner of Ireland in 1982 brought an end to the making of pots, but fresh inspiration was on hand thanks to the area's enticing mixture of impressive geological formations, abundant Neolithic remains and the rugged Atlantic seaboard. The coastline of North Beara, where Kingerlee settled, is separated from the south side of the peninsula by the Slieve Miskish Mountains and has only been served by roads for the last century and a half. Prior to 1840, explorers wanting to reach the Kerry side of the peninsula were better advised to do so by ship than to attempt the journey on foot. The opening of the copper mines at Allihies in 1810 brought brief prosperity to the area, prompting Thomas Crofton Croker, writing in 1824, to note that "The place where, but a few years since, the barren and rocky mountains could scarcely sustain the lives of a few half-starved sheep, is now the scene of busy and useful employment". The mines closed for the last time in 1962, having been brought to the attention of the world twenty years earlier through Daphne du Maurier's novel *Hungry Hill*. The villages of Allihies and Eyeries apart, however, this district of Ireland is but sparsely populated.

Not one to shy away from adventure, the artist moved into a remote cottage at Cleanagh near Allihies that had no electricity, no bathroom, no television and no telephone. Moreover, it was located at the end of a one-and-a-half mile farm track. Without a car, self-sufficiency was the order of the day. Kingerlee grew his own vegetables – potatoes, leeks, parsnips, radishes, spring onions and salad, but winter greens were a waste of time as the tops got blown off in the strong winds. In the winter they would light the paraffin lamps at three o'clock in the afternoon and occupy themselves by playing patience, listening to the radio or painting. Bags of coal and heavy gas bottles were delivered to the end of the track and would then have to be hauled manually up the hill to the house. Life was far from easy, one might even say primitive, but the compensating factor was the unspoilt and romantically isolated location, with a sweep of rocky hills to the rear (part of which was formerly used as a mass rock), and the island-strewn mouth of Kenmare Bay to the fore, stretching across to the Kerry mountains.

One of the most important pictures completed at Cleanagh is *Lingam (Just the Whisper)*, dating from the artist's fourth year at this location. The colours and forms are a summation of various experiences and beliefs, reflecting the artist's cross-cultural awareness. In Hindu religion the worshipers of Siva have a great stone, or lingam, that symbolises the deity as the one great unity, the one eye. The stone, which also has phallic connotations, can be seen at the left of the composition, looking not dissimilar to some of the megalithic monuments found in the west of Ireland. The reference in the picture's title to a whisper may refer to the silent communication of the stone, or perhaps to the mysterious music that the artist heard quite clearly one day when working alone in the middle of a field.

Lingam (Just the Whisper)
1986, oil on canvas, 66 cms x 92 cms

The allusions in *Lingam* and other contemporary paintings were generally arrived at by suppressing conscious thought. An idea, an image or a story might supply the initial spark of inspiration. Then, through the process of working, other ideas would surface, taking their place alongside the aesthetic judgements that determine what colours and what brushmarks should be used. By introducing greater spontaneity into the creative process Kingerlee gave the viewer complete freedom to interpret the painting on his/her own terms. S/he is not dependant on the artist to decode meaning from an image.

Another painting of the same year, *Tree in Prague*, is more obviously a landscape, but the trigger of inspiration did not come from a visit to the Czech capital. Instead it was inspired by an American acquaintance's story of how he traced his roots to Prague. The painting is therefore not a landscape in the traditional sense of the word, it is not a topographical record of a real place necessitating a physical journey for the purpose of documenting it accurately. Instead the work of art stems from an act of psychic and emotional projection. *Tree in Prague* demonstrates how, as early as the mid-1980s, Kingerlee had already begun to question received pictorial conventions and posit alternative approaches to the genre of landscape.

Following the move in 1987 to more comfortable accommodation with mains electricity, the staging of several successful exhibitions of his work in Dublin and Belfast enabled him to build a separate studio six years later. He has continued to live and work there to this day, all the while extending and enriching what is arguably the most productive period of his career to date.

In *Dancing on the Shore*, an oil painting of 1990, he adopted a simpler, more schematic approach than the one he had favoured in his Cleanagh pictures. The landscape is reduced to three horizontal strips of green, red and cream, each of them thinly painted and separated by areas of bare canvas. By blurring the leading edge of the green strip the artist manages to convey an impression of low-lying cloud or mist, as of a headland glimpsed on the far side of a body of water. The painting's title further reinforces the sense of a specific locality, which functions as a setting for the two figures. These, however, are pushed to the edge of the composition, allowing the stretch of shoreline to occupy centre-stage. The colours and shapes remain sufficiently undefined for there to be a tension, a duality, between the painting as

Dancing on the Shore
1990, oil on canvas, 25 cms x 33 cms

land- or sea-scape, and the painting as abstract composition. This ambiguity is, in itself, a reflection of the Beara scene, where the elements – land, water, air – come together, separate and dissolve with startling rapidity.

The completion of the new studio with its own entrance from the garden gave Kingerlee a dedicated working area for the first time in his life, together with much needed storage space. Another benefit was the psychological freedom to reconsider his working methods. The acrylics he had been producing recently gave way to oil paintings, and he abandoned ready-mixed paints having decided to mix his own colours. He grew dissatisfied with earlier pictures that were hanging around the studio, but rather than simply throwing them out, his abhorrence of waste led him to try painting over their tops and making them into new pictures. Canvases and boards treated in this way would be set aside to dry for a period of days or even weeks, depending on the thickness of the new coat of paint. When he pulled them off the shelf again to add fresh colour he was intrigued by the fact that their past histories remained visible, showing through and influencing the character of the new 'skin' in the same way that the growth rings of a tree are reflected in the outer bark. The artist asked himself what would happen if another layer was added, not as a uniform coat necessarily, but applied rather to certain parts only. Some areas would select themselves, as it were, by virtue of being more heavily built up and thus taking the paint first from the proffered palette knife or brush. Other areas would be less subject to random effects, as when the artist's aesthetic judgement engenders a reaction to what has already been put down in the way of colours, marks and gestures.

The combination of conscious and unconscious actions opened up endless and exciting possibilities, which multiplied as new layers were added and the surface became more heavily textured. Kingerlee had stumbled on a whole new way of working with oil paint. Where many painters would have failed to recognise the method's potential or else shrunk back in fear at the thought of being branded as strange or 'other', he chose to make it the new foundation stone of his art. He risked all in the pursuit of a new form of landscape painting.

Anyone who has painted in oil colours knows that a picture can take anything up to a week or more to dry, depending on the ambient temperature. A complex painting worked over a number of different sessions requires even more patience, if the messy effect of wet paint blending with wet paint of a different colour is to be avoided. The sort of multi-layering that John Kingerlee had embarked on demanded months and often years of drying time. Hence he often has up to a hundred or more works in progress in the studio, all in varying states of completion.

A typical painting session begins with the mixing of half a dozen or so powdered pigments with linseed oil on a palette (he mail orders pigments from a long established firm of artists' colourmen located close to London's British Museum in premises that look like a Victorian apothecary's shop). The smell and feel of the materials as they are blended together can be seen as a technical warm-up session, a breaking of the gestural 'ice' before real painting begins. The mounds of mixed pigment stand well proud of the palette, looking like a miniature mountain range. Next the artist chooses a batch of dry pictures of a similar size, places them on his workbench, and from a standing position applies a fresh layer of colour to each of them in turn (previously unpainted surfaces will be primed first with a coat of emulsion). He prefers to work on paintings of modest dimensions, generally not more than eighteen inches across. His tools of choice are palette knives and decorating brushes, these latter being held vertically so as to allow the paint to be stippled onto the surface. He has a stock of about fifteen different colours at his disposal, which include the exotically named Phthalo Turquoise, Pozzuoli Red, Oriental Blue and Coral Red (at £20 per 250g bag the latter is the most expensive pigment he uses). As befits a painter who is so in tune with the landscape, he is particularly fond of the earth colours, for example Golden Ochre, Burnt Umber and Indian Red.

A single picture might end up with as many as fifty coats of paint, almost creating the effect of a relief sculpture. The three-dimensional aspect is sometimes bolstered by the addition of sand, itself a component of the landscape, to the paint mixture, or alternatively by prising the crust off the top of a mound of pigment on his palette and incorporating it into the still wet surface of a picture. If one were able to view the layers of one of these paintings in cross-section, the analogy with geological strata would surely be striking.

A predilection for heavily impasted and textured paint is not, of course, a novelty in the history of western art. From Rembrandt to late Monet, Dubuffet to Auerbach, it is easy to find distinguished practitioners of the loaded brush and knife approach. Kingerlee has been influenced by Braque, who stressed that he worked with materials rather than ideas, and who not only ground his own colours but also mixed sand with his pigments. He also feels an affinity with the Cobra artists of the late 1940s and early 1950s, especially the Danish painter Asger Jorn (1914–73), whose sense of play and use of instinctive forms continue to inspire him. Jorn's technique, however, was very much of its time in that it shared with other Cobra, Art Brut and Tachist painters a desire to overthrow all manifestations of cultural refinement: hence expressive and violent brushstrokes dominated their work. Kingerlee, on the other hand, paints in a more methodical fashion, avoiding impetuous and crude effects at all costs. It has to be remembered that his surfaces generally become so three-dimensional, so undercut and varied in texture that they provide a far from ideal footing for the rapidly executed gesture. Subtlety and denial of the ego are the order of the day, as can be seen in a picture such as *Heads and Fields III* with its finely gradated tonal and chromatic transitions. Even the ghostly head that emerges from the red paint on the right-hand side of the composition appears calm, dignified, as if he is imagining the scene to his left.

Heads and Fields III
2003, oil on canvas, 40 cms x 50 cms

That the artist sees these seemingly abstract paintings as landscapes is confirmed by the titles of his exhibited works. The catalogue of an exhibition in 1999, for example, lists paintings that are generically described as landscapes, in addition to pieces with more specific references to the natural world such as *Where the Fungi grew, Warwickshire Flood* and *Stones in the Wood Lauragh*. However, we will search in vain for visible signs of any of these objects in the pictures they allude to, for the titling is done afterwards as a literary adjunct to the prevailing mood or disposition of shapes within a given work. The catalogue of an exhibition that took place in 2002 reproduces pictures named *Gift Day* and *Soft Landscape*, titles that are indicative of a more general aim to instil an atmosphere of calmness and serenity in the work. This meditative quality forms a direct corollary to the painter's deeply held thoughts and beliefs. To express them in paint, he combines subdued colours with an indefiniteness of shape and form. While he is not averse to using brighter colours in his work, a restrained palette makes more logical sense when it is compared with the marginal situation of the Beara peninsula, where the clarity of what one sees is so dependent on the weather.

Peeks is a typical example of the way the artist re-interprets and re-invents the landscape genre. The glutinous accretions of pigment successfully evoke the textures and colours of earth and rock. By juxtaposing gritty sections with more subtly rendered areas, the artist also imbues the pigment with an ability to melt away, to dissolve visually to the point where it is replaced by an illusion of space and the eye is carried back through the layers of pigment. The journey the eye takes through the painting is very similar to that of exploring a landscape on foot. Half-formed shapes come in and out of focus, too vaguely defined for us to be able to identify them. The artist's skilled handling of tonal contrasts conveys the impression of an inner radiance, of a soft light pervading the space, enframing it almost as it draws and holds our gaze.

While the artist is possessed of good colour sense and every so often lets rip on a landscape using dazzling chromatic fireworks, the general trend in recent years has been for a more understated formula. This is especially true of the paintings he refers to as "white-outs", which were started in the late 1990s and have become a more regular feature of his output since 2002. In these works the framing devices, trees and shorelines of earlier landscapes give way to much more diffuse forms.

The challenge of working with a very limited range of colours is one that appeals to the artist, inevitably prompting comparison with other practitioners of the white-on-white discipline such as Whistler and Le Brocquy. In Kingerlee's hands the subject of the artist's scrutiny seems to be not so much the landscape itself as the atmosphere that envelopes it, hence a more appropriate comparison would be with some of the late works of Turner and Monet, for example the latter's *Haystacks* series. When we look at a picture such as *The Rich Landscape*, we almost feel as if we are lying on our backs gazing up at white cumulus clouds

Peeks
1999–2004, oil on card, 21 cms x 26 cms

The Rich Landscape
1995–2003, oil on board, 36 cms x 48 cms

drifting past, or alternatively peering at the vague shapes of trees and hedges through early morning mist clinging to a river. A remarkable quietness and sense of calm exudes from these works, which seem to celebrate purity of the mind as much as purity of nature. Painterly, self-proclaiming gestures would be entirely out of place in this context. Instead, the pigment has the appearance of having been deposited and eroded by natural processes. It is as if the myriad scrapings of the palette knife and stabs of the brush have left behind a sort of painterly glacial moraine. What we are seeing in the finished white-outs is arrested movement, a still point reached after prolonged activity.

Many owners of the artist's pictures become very attached to them and place great store in their capacity to provide an antidote to stress. To cite but one case in point:

> " I've always said, if someone's ill in bed and they had one of my pictures on the wall, they'd have a good companion to help the days go by … It was a great thrill for me to discover that a picture a dealer had bought from me called The Well was seen by a woman who popped into the gallery having just discovered that her husband had been unfaithful to her. She was very depressed and was planning to go off to the countryside to commit suicide. She looked at the picture, bought it, didn't commit suicide. It saved somebody's life – that's better than yards of art criticism and aesthetics. I'd like the work to have that quality, so that it gives life to people and it functions as a weapon against the negativity and destruction of the times in which we live. "

Kingerlee was, and still is, enormously touched by this tribute. To him it is tangible proof that his paintings are capable of communicating the life-affirming, uplifting messages he is looking for. In his daily life he never ceases to give thanks for the wonder of existence, to rejoice in the things we take for granted:

> " Just to be here is a miracle. I'd like to communicate that to people because I feel that more and more as this age progresses we're loosing that sense of the miraculousness of being here … I'd like all my paintings to be on the side of the anti-consumer society brigade, to be for human beings, for a good life, for the creatures of the earth. We are so blessed to be here, the whole planet is a garden. "

CHAPTER FOUR

DIFFUSED MATTER

WHEN ASKED whether he sees himself as an abstract painter, Kingerlee replies that it is not a dialectic that has much meaning for him. In other words, he does not see his art as a pendulum swinging between the twin polarities of abstraction and figuration. At the end of the day, he is a maker of surfaces that are articulated using a language of lines, colours and textures. Recognisable forms will spontaneously appear, get covered over and then be resurrected through the extended creative process. What comes out at the other end is a resolution of this activity, not unlike the calm that returns to the surface of a lake after a stone has been dropped into it.

Nonetheless, Kingerlee's oeuvre does break down into a number of broad thematic groupings, which are reflected in the structure of the preceding chapters. He likes to work on a body of pictures in unison, employing the same techniques and materials to bring the whole group gradually towards completion, whether it comprises gothics, grids, heads or landscapes. By so doing he avoids wastage of materials and effort, whilst keeping at bay the vanity that so often pertains when an artist devotes all his energies to the completion of a single picture. To watch him painting is to realise, with some degree of shock initially, just how unconscious his methods are. He works fluidly and without hesitation, picking up unfinished pictures, briskly adding another layer of paint to them and then putting them down again with a confidence born of decades of experience. The tools and colours he has to hand, the gestures he uses, are applied to perhaps five or six pictures in turn, all bearing a family relationship, yet each somehow managing to emerge with its own distinct identity.

So is there a family of abstract pictures? In a sense, everything the artist paints is abstracted, to a greater or lesser degree, but the question should perhaps be re-phrased by asking whether some of his techniques are more inherently resistant towards figuration than others. This penultimate chapter attempts to answer that question, although it should first be emphasised that he never resorts to experimentation as an end in itself. Expanding his knowledge contributes to his artistic vitality, even if this means trialling methods which occasionally misfire and are not developed any further.

The painting *Overcrowded Market* of 1967 is covered in an all-over pattern of bright, intricately worked colours, giving the appearance

Overcrowded Market
1967, oil on board, 50 cms x 65 cms

of a mosaic or tapestry. Is it a section of the earth's crust viewed from outer space, or alternatively an underwater view of corals in some warmer sea than our own? Whatever the picture may or may not represent, one senses that the richly textured pigment constitutes an act of homage to the natural world, set down deliberately and systematically, without resorting to showy, self-proclaiming gestures. In the context of the artist's predominantly figurative work from this period the picture is unusual, but it does anticipate some of the methods he would develop twenty and more years into the future.

One of Kingerlee's most purely abstract paintings comprises a flat pink colour field with a large vertical 'zip' going up its left-hand side. Dating from 1970, it recalls the work of Lucio Fontana in its elegant simplicity, but again it is a one-off, totally different in feel and execution from anything done before or after. In 1972 he made some pen drawings using hieroglyphic motifs, but their taut execution was the antithesis of the spontaneity he has since been at pains to preserve. The mid-1980s saw him paint the occasional lyrical abstract work such as *Lingam (Just the Whisper)* (p. 89), aided by a new freedom of colour and form, but he still held back from a more far reaching exploration of non-figurative subject matter. However, this diffidence was destined to end soon.

In 1988 the artist converted to Islam. The repercussions of this event, which can only be described as a major turning point, were felt as much in the artist's work as in his life. Since that date the practice of incorporating recognisable images into his paintings has gradually decreased. Forms have become more diaphanous, more generalised and abstracted, rendering them ambiguous through compositional simplifications and the overlaying of one form on top of another, as seen for example in *Thinking of Australia* and *The wounded dog recovers*, both painted in 1988. In more recent works the distinction between one form and another has been eroded even further, by relying purely on variations of colour and tone to achieve this effect, as opposed to drawn contours.

One side-effect of this highly painterly solution is that it results in a conflation of the foreground and background of the picture. And in some works, notably the white-outs, individual forms have disappeared completely, engulfed as they are by a homogenous continuum. The transformation did not happen overnight. Instead it was an incremental change phased over a period of about fifteen years. Underpinning it is a mystical belief in the 'Unity of all Being', one of the key concepts of Sufism, the Muslim faith to which the artist converted. Just as the ego has to be annihilated in order to seek union with God, in the same way the transcription of detail needs to be avoided so that it does not hinder our perception of the interdependency of creation. The dilemma facing the artist is that he still has to work with the visible in order to conjure a sense of the invisible. By eliding form, colour and space, Kingerlee hopes to allude to the greater Unity. This is true of his landscapes as well as his grid paintings, whilst the recent Heads have also lost some of their former definition.

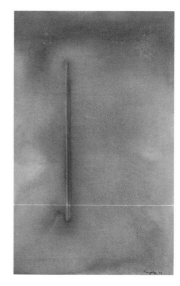

Zip Painting, Cornwall
1970, acrylic on calico, 84 cms x 53 cms

Grid of Artist's Life
1972, pen and ink on paper, 36 cms x 28 cms

The Wounded Dog Recovers
1988, oil on canvas, 42 cms x 62 cms

Beara Landscape
2005, oil on board, 30 cms x 43 cms

Tribute Four
2001, acrylic on board, 14 cms x 19 cms

Another way of describing this shift would be to say that it is about moving from the particular to the universal, from microcosm to macrocosm. Visible reality is a veil, tantalising and seductive perhaps, but the real substance of creation, of life itself, is found beneath this superficial layer. Terms such as object and subject loose all meaning in any analysis of these paintings. A language that is grounded in the assumed duality of perceiver and perceived cannot deal with a Reality that is both all-encompassing and immeasurable.

Rub-backs

Since 1997 the artist's growing commitment to abstraction has resulted in the development of two new bodies of work: the so-called 'rub-backs' and the 'grids'. The former tend to be small paintings which are executed in acrylics. They come about through experimentation, by allowing knowledge to be delivered to him by chance, and then capitalising on the most interesting discoveries. One of the advantages of working in acrylic is the much shorter drying time. Three or four layers of paint can be built up quite quickly, interleaving a series of contrasting colours without any risk of messy or uneven coverage. By rubbing the topmost layer hard, by physically scouring it, parts of the underlying colours are exposed, either with total clarity or else shining through a grainy or filmy residue of another colour. The effect could be nuanced still further by holding the pictures under running water whilst abrading their surfaces.

Some of Kingerlee's most sensuously rich works have been made using this unusual technique. Each cell of one of the rub-backs can be viewed as a miniature landscape, or then again it could be a windowpane, a frame from a film or a comic book story, or the weathered remnants of an abandoned advertising hoarding. The feathering and drawing out of the pigment will often convey an impression of movement, like the blurred forms of figures and posters seen through the glass of an underground train as it pulls away from the platform.

While the artist readily acknowledges that his experiences of living in London fed into these paintings, it is not the swinging London of the 'sixties that he draws on, but rather the seedy underbelly that is the domain of the graffiti artist, the drunk and the homeless person. A former squatter himself, he is well equipped to appreciate and distil the grittier poetry of the streets and subways:

" On a visit to London in 1986, at Camden Town and Tottenham Court Road tube stations, I was really taken by the courage of the graffiti artists who put themselves in dangerous situations when crossing the line to make an artistic expression. I was also fascinated by the billboards themselves with their layer upon layer of pigment. I have resurrected some of these memories as one of the components of my rub-backs. "

The source is never translated verbatim into the work, however. The artist's sensibility compresses the weather-beaten, time-stained and spray-canned surfaces of his beloved underground into the reductively created textures and colours of pictures that are no larger than thirty centimetres across.

Grids

Kingerlee began making grids in 1996–97 inspired partly by a visit to the hill of Tara in County Meath, seat of the high kings of Ireland. The appearance of the tumuli may not have provided him with a direct source of inspiration, yet the presence underground of so much buried history and power could have impacted on his work nonetheless, in the sense that it paralleled on a large scale the accumulated strata of his oil paintings. His painting process is, if one thinks about it, a sort of reverse archaeology. By adapting the technique to suit the format of a grid, he made the evolution of the painting more obvious and allowed the passage of time itself to be an integral part of the picture. When we look at one of the grids we are not experiencing a painting in the singular, but rather the evidence of as many as fifty or more, piled one on top of the other.

The very first grids emerged as drawings, but it was not long before the artist imposed the same discipline on his oils, shaping and blending the pigment into more or less even rectangles which he set out in rows, butting up against each other at first but later with gaps in between. The linear matrix, which is imposed at the beginning of the painting process, was inspired by the early Cubist work of Picasso and Braque (John particularly likes Braque's allusion to the collaboration with Picasso as being "like two mountaineers roped together"). Colours are laid on with brushes initially, working from strong bright tints through to more muted shades:

> " the canvases become more and more subtle as they progress. A lot of white has gone into them and the very bright colours become no more than delicate traces. I really like the subtlety of reduced colour. "

In the later stages the method of application switches to a combination of palette knife work and stippling. The process is analogous to that of making a collage, in the sense that when he is working on a grid he applies 'pieces' of paint in regular shapes using a palette knife, almost as if they were small rectangles of card and paper:

> " I am trying to build up a plaque, a raised textured surface. As each coat is added each plaque is more enriched, more and more figurative – landscapes, animals, buildings; sometimes the obvious image isn't there – sometimes abstract – never a pure accident. The minute it seems a pure accident it's no longer that but has become a conscious choice. "

Early Grid Painting
1998, oil on board, 20 cms x 28 cms

Grid Drawing in Granada
2005, pastel and mixed media on paper, 23 cms x 30 cms

Some of the layers are worked wet into wet, allowing the different colours to partially blend. The results are as unpredictable as they are exciting, for each cell will respond differently depending on the thickness of the pigment and the pressure with which it has been applied. The process is akin to a gardener tending his borders, and in the same way that soil will crumble and collapse, so the edges of the little 'heaps' of paint spill over, softening the grid's geometry. In *Grid of Life*, painted between 1997 and 2003 (p. 206), the edges of some of the rectangles have broken down completely and merged with the background as well as with each other, while there is also considerable unevenness in the proportions of the repeated shapes. The whole composition seems to flicker in and out of focus, the pattern forming, dissolving and reforming, in the same way that the Cubists broke forms down and rendered their interpenetration one with another.

Not all the grids have the shimmering effect of *Grid of Life*. Many of them are flatter and more regular in appearance, incorporating rectangles that do not 'bleed' nearly so much at the edges. Clearly the grid format allows for infinite variation and is never allowed to become a mere formula. In *If I was a man I'd be knocking down my own door*, dating from 2004, the general composition and the colours seem to be suggestive of buildings, packed closely together and rising in rows up a hillside. Other grids have drier and harsher textures that are more reminiscent of walls, and in one example (p. 207) the gaps between the 'building blocks' have even been closed so that they butt up against each other, with the edges defined by protruding ridges of paint. In March 2005, whilst staying in Granada, he completed his first acrylic grids, employing a palette of nine colours that included no less than three different yellows. He particularly favours yellow for its ability to inject an inner glow or radiance into his compositions, the effect being reminiscent of that found in the most painterly of Turner's late seascapes.

Although the artist regards the grid cells as miniature pictures, teetering on the brink between nature and abstraction, they retain the illusion of being located in three-dimensional space. Some viewers see figures in the pictures, whilst others point to similarities with the *Harmonies* of Paul Klee and the architectonic abstracts of Nicholas de Stael. Rather than taking an all too narrow view of Kingerlee's grids, however, perhaps we should recognise that these unique works are open to interpretation. At the end of the day we have to work with the evidence presented to our senses. Then we may notice, for example, that the rectangles advance and recede in space, as if suspended or hovering at varying distances from the picture plane. The eye travels not only to right and left and up and down, but also backwards and forwards, feeling its way through the gaps between the shapes as well as through the shapes themselves, for sometimes we cannot be sure that the patches are not windows or openings, rather than solid forms. A sense of spatial infinity and ambiguity is thus engendered by these works, tempered by a pervasive tranquillity.

If I was a man I'd be knocking down my own door
2004, oil on paper, 19 cms x 28 cms

Grid in Granada IV
2005, acrylic on canvas, 52 cms x 40 cms

Gothics

Like the rub-backs, the gothics stem from a process of experimentation, and again like the other series they are painted in acrylic colours. The term 'gothic' is the artist's own description and was suggested by the predominance of black which is a common feature of the series, although he was never entirely happy with the word's nightmarish overtones. Indeed, far from being in the least sinister, some of the gothics are distinctly light in tone and mood.

Gothic
2005, oil on board, 36 cms x 48 cms

The series proper was started in 2004, but earlier one-offs using similar methods can be found, one of which bears a date of 1997. For the most part they are totally abstract, resisting figuration as determinedly as Jackson Pollock's 'drip' paintings, albeit on a much smaller scale and lacking the psychotic intensity that underpins his handling of pigment. In order to make them, Kingerlee works with one colour at a time, applying paint in a network of seemingly random marks across the image. The calligraphic touches become progressively denser and more interwoven as fresh colours are worked in.

Shadowy figures can sometimes be detected within the welter of colours: a head-and-shoulders or a cloaked traveller, perhaps (see p. 157). But even when this is not the case, the dynamic surfaces that are such a dominant feature of the gothics seem to echo the liveliness of public spaces. The same vital spark that he has witnessed on the streets of Fez and Hyderabad, London and Paris, the same life-force that binds and connects us one to another, is here channelled into the rhythmic movements of his paintbrush.

CHAPTER FIVE

THOUGHTS ON PAPER

The Flower Lady
1982, watercolour, pen and ink on paper,
20 cms x 16 cms

Flight into Egypt
1994, mixed media on paper,
20 cms x 14 cms

THE DISCIPLINE of drawing enjoys primary status in the work of John Kingerlee, on whom it seems to exert what can only be described as a compulsive fascination, apparent in the fact that he devotes at least as much time to it and to the making of collages as he does to painting. In the course of his career the quantity of drawings he has produced runs to many thousands and must exceed his output of paintings. The convenience and lightness of graphic materials (pencil, paper, pen, ink) are well suited to his itinerant existence, and in one sense the works on paper form a visual diary of the places he has visited, the people he has met and the thoughts that have preoccupied him on his journeys. He takes small notebooks with him wherever he goes and will make drawings even while he is sitting in the passenger seat of a moving car. Back at home, he requisitions the kitchen table and turns the space into a laboratory for cooking up drawings, collages and mixed media works, often working simultaneously on dozens of items and continuing without a break well into the small hours of the night. In this way, a distinct physical space is reserved for the works on paper, which never migrate into the painting studio except as finished pieces requiring storage. But even though drawing and painting are not linked in his working routine, he brings to each medium the same respect for materials and the same insistence on good making.

Most of the artist's drawings are meticulously signed and dated, allowing us to chart the main stylistic and thematic shifts in his career, and at the same time identify similarities and contrasts with the painted oeuvre. For example, in terms of subject matter the drawings tend to feature more multi-figure compositions, more scenes with animals and fewer landscapes than the oil paintings. The drawn figures also reveal their origins in everyday life more clearly than their painted equivalents. This is apparent from the frequency with which Kingerlee captures and preserves observational details in his drawings, such as people wearing hats at jaunty angles or holding flowers, a child straining on her mother's hand, a knife-grinder plying his trade on a busy street in Fez, or a person riding a mule. In the collages these representational triggers are replaced by recycled ephemera such as postage stamps bearing images of birds and small photos of film-stars, which ultimately serve the same purpose: to inject spontaneity and vitality into the work.

The energised character of Kingerlee's drawings and collages is also attributable, at least in part, to the fact that graphic media are not conducive to the sort of prolonged gestation that is demanded by his oil paintings, with their multi-layered surfaces. The oils thus tend to yield images that are more universalised and abstracted. This can be demonstrated by comparing the drawn heads in which the features are mapped out boldly using line, with the painted heads which immediately seem more ethereal and, in the case of very recent productions, almost appear to float disembodied in space.

A typical Kingerlee drawing will combine a range of different media, often including some colour washes in acrylic or watercolour. *Walking the Dog*, 2003 even has some sand mixed in with the pigment to create texture and relief. As a consequence, the foreground of this drawing takes on the density of a rock-like substance, in complete contrast to the rest of the image which combines fluid calligraphy in the drawing of the figure with semi-transparent washes that allow the underlying pencil hatchings to show through. The rapidity of the pencil and pen work suggests movement, not only of the figure but also of the space surrounding him, as if rain is falling or the clouds are being driven by strong winds. There is a doodle-like quality to some of the pencil lines, inspired perhaps by the artist's love of graffiti and the random scribbles people make when they are on the telephone. The shorthand marks convey the essentials of the scene, leaving the viewer to fill in the missing details. What mission is the striding figure embarked upon? Where is he going? Is the animal on the horizon a dog, a goat or a donkey? What is the kite-like shape in the upper left-hand corner? Why is the terrain so inhospitable? It is almost as if we have been given one frame of a film, one small part of a much bigger story to which we are not privy. The drawing is an enticing fragment, an invitation to project ourselves into the scene and engage our imaginations.

Stories and jokes are grist to the Kingerlee mill: he takes as much delight in telling them as he does in listening to them. Drawing presents him with a language of images rather than words, a vocabulary of spontaneous marks, gestures, tones and empty spaces which he can use to communicate his message. Like any good story-teller he will ad lib, giving free reign to his own creative imagination, and at the same time responding intuitively to unforeseen circumstances. Another analogy would be with the composer who writes a piece of music comprising a theme and variations. The theme of *Walking the Dog* is the interaction between human beings and quadrupeds, a subject he has explored in countless variations, some of them ambiguous whilst others are immediately recognisable as a man or woman walking a dog on a lead. In some of the variants the animal assumes larger proportions and is transformed into a donkey, on the back of which sits a person or occasionally a large bird. Sometimes the story will take on the character of a myth or fairy-tale, as when, for example, a giant bird with an egg at its feet has a close encounter with a human bystander.

Walking the Dog
2003, mixed media with sand on paper, 15 cms x 20 cms

Elegant Lady
1997, watercolour and mixed media on paper,
20 cms x 14 cms

Italo Memory 1
2003, collage and mixed media on paper,
24 cms x 32 cms

The Young Picasso at Gosol
2003, collage and mixed media on card, 30 cms x 20 cms

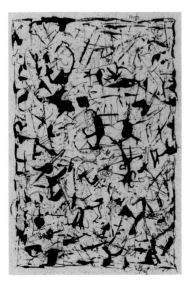

Crowded Place
1995, pen and ink on Indian paper, 27 cms x 17 cms

Other drawings take their cue from events the artist has witnessed or been moved by. These might be incidents in which he has been an active player, such as the joy on discovering that his wife was pregnant with twins (see p. 21) or the sorrow resulting from a pointless row with a friend (see *The fruit-less argument*, 2002). In 2003 he dedicated a series of drawings to the memory of a boyhood friend, Italo, who became a test pilot and lost his life while still young in an air accident. Looking beyond his own personal experience, a tragicomic episode or tale might capture his imagination, as in the caricature-like *Taking the Husband's Head to the Market* (1997). Other subjects are taken from the arena of modern art and international affairs, such as *The Young Picasso at Gosol* (2003), and the 40th anniversary of the assassination of President Kennedy. He commemorated the 2001 destruction of New York's Twin Towers with a collage incorporating a poignant newspaper photograph of a young girl holding a thermometer in her mouth (p. 265).

Kingerlee often uses drawing as a testing ground for new ideas and techniques, capitalising on its ability to deliver results much more speedily than painting. By keeping his art alive to untried materials and methods, he lets chance, the unconscious, influence the character and positioning of his marks, thereby avoiding any danger of the stagnation that results from a formulaic approach. In this he is very similar to Jean-Michel Basquiat, an artist whose work he greatly admires:

" With Basquiat's drawings it is as if they had been on the floor and people had walked over them, a brush had splashed on them, and then he'd done a drawing on them. All these little chance marks from daily life are allowed to enter into the work. I much prefer that to the finished chic with which one does this delicate sensitive thing. That's got its place too, but the urge to achieve it can become like a mania. I find it so thrilling when an artist such as Basquiat somehow arrives at a drawing by transforming a grotty bit of paper. And that's an element in my work here. Everything's all over the place – that falls off, it gets slightly damp, so it becomes part of the picture, and so on. "

In 1994–95 Kingerlee made a series of black ink drawings comprising webs of spidery, seemingly random lines which were partially obscured by thicker 'blots'. The creative spark on this occasion came from the interplay between two different kinds of calligraphic marks, and the opportunity they afforded to insert recognisable shapes into the web, such as figures, heads, clock faces, mountains and hearts pierced by arrows. These drawings bear comparison with the rhythmic calligraphy of Arabic script, just as they embody the graphic vitality that underscores the best graffiti art. On occasions he has even gone out of his way to admire and photograph graffiti, notably on a visit to London (en route to India) in 1986.

Sometimes an existing printed image or page will be given a new identity by being over-drawn or over-painted. One of the earliest surviving examples of this technique is a postcard of the Matterhorn that was addressed collectively to 'The Waysiders' (squatters) at 56 Grafton Way, London in 1976. The artist applied paint over the top of the photographic image on the card, transforming it into a bearded face viewed in profile, wearing a hat that was once the snow-capped peak. To the right of the head a small figure of a child with outstretched arms has been added, whilst the trees framing the view have been spotted with red and white paint to represent blossom. By adapting a 'found' image in this way, Kingerlee calls to mind Salvador Dali's famous collage from the 1930s featuring a box filled with puppies superimposed over an Alpine scene with skiing figures. For the most part, however, he avoids the visual trickery of the Surrealists. There is, instead, a touch of iconoclasm in his habit of painting over reproductions of works by other artists, such as Ana Maria Pacheco and Lucian Freud. In 2003 he subjected a book of etchings by Freud to this treatment, using a brush loaded with paint to systematically convert each Freud portrait into a totally fresh and original Kingerlee head. It will come as no surprise to learn that he is not a fan of his fellow painter's brutally honest transcriptions of the human form.

Kingerlee also subjects other 'found' materials to transformative procedures – for example lithographs of standing stones by his former neighbour Tim Goulding (which they both painted over), as well as pages from diaries, auction catalogues and novels. The choice of books sometimes seem random (for example *Rachel Ray* and *The American Senator* by Anthony Trollope), whilst others carry personal resonances notably *The Ringer* by Edgar Wallace, a thriller his father used to read out loud to him as a child. In some of the book-works he preserves the integrity of the printed page, allowing the letter and word forms to show through his boldly calligraphic, crayoned design. Parts of a machine-made multiple are thus rendered unique by the touch of the artist's hand. This technique is developed even further in the 'rip-and-tear' works, which rely on an adaptation of the monotype process. Here paint is applied over a printed page which is then pressed onto the surface of the dry facing page, prior to pulling the two surfaces apart. Depending on the quantity of paint used and the amount of time the pages are held together, they will not separate cleanly, the tearing action leaving rips in both pieces of paper. The effects are highly unpredictable and complex, as surfaces, colours, words and printed images are subjected to the vagaries of chance. Sometimes an entire double-page spread will be presented as one work that is more or less symmetrical in design. In *Circle*, a serene grey and white rip-and-tear work dating from 2002, the two halves of the image were united by the simple device of the painted outline of a circle, an emblem of reason that sits confidently above the underlying chaos.

Books aside, Kingerlee's affection for printed ephemera impels him to incorporate them into collages, painting over and around them until

Matterhorn Postcard
1976, collage and mixed media on postcard,
15 cms x 10 cms

Head of Bruce Bernard
paint-over in Lucian Freud etchings book

Sotheby's Series
2003, collage and mixed media on printed paper,
24 cms x 17 cms

Circle
2000, mixed media on book pages, 15 cms x 23 cms

For Guillaume Apollinaire
2002, collage and mixed media on hotel bill,
21 cms x 16 cms

Memory of Eleanor Boardman
2004, collage and oil on board, 23 cms x 18 cms

the two types of imagery coexist harmoniously. The flotsam and jetsam he chooses generally replicates in printed form the principal subjects of his paintings, in other words they feature animals, human figures and stories. Among his most cherished and frequently occurring items are postage stamps bearing images of birds, cigarette packets, hotel bills, cinema tickets, London Underground tickets and maps, and black-and-white photographs of film divas of the past. A collage of 2004 even incorporates a tape measure. Others breathe new life into old drawings he has grown tired of, by bringing them into a new relationship with other collaged items and passages of paint (the process recalls the 'reused' or 'defigured' works Asger Jorn made during 1959–62 by painting on top of conventional nineteenth-century pictures acquired from junk shops).

Often the 'found' materials will not be used straightaway, some even being picked up, magpie-like, for no apparent reason other than the ritual of saving them from destruction. In 2003 he used an attractive butcher's receipt from the Cornish port of Mevagissey, issued in June 1965 for a pound and a half of mincemeat, to make a collage that also included a cut-out male figure of the type found on doors of public toilets (see p. 261). The printed image of a heifer that embellishes the receipt is a poignant reminder of a time when we did our shopping in the high street and shopkeepers prided themselves on giving personal service.

Kingerlee's respect for these mini time capsules often induces him to paint around rather than over them, as can be seen for example in *Memory of Eleanor Boardman* and *Inside Out* (p. 268), both completed in 2004. The accessible images of birds, movie stars and prancing horses that adorn these humble, reclaimed objects provide us with a secure foothold in the everyday, however abstract the rest of the work might be. Every collage he makes is effectively an act of homage to the key image. He tends to avoid the proliferations of clippings that create an all-over effect in the collages of Kurt Schwitters, for example, the Dadaist and inventor of *Merz* (art from discarded materials), despite reserving the greatest admiration for the German artist's work. Nor does he essay the measured architectonic structures of Cubist collages, with their interpenetrations of volumes and spaces. On the rare occasions when he does reassemble a plethora of torn shards of paper, they will be pasted into a collective shape such as a geometrically configured, striding figure (see p. 273).

Many other instances of Kingerlee's technical experimentation could be cited, but the purpose here has been to identify some of his most common practices. In the interest of providing a balanced account, attention also needs to be drawn to that other vital source of inspiration for the works on paper: the time he has spent away from his homes in Cornwall and West Cork, travelling to other places. These trips not only enable him to collect raw material for the collages, they also bring him into contact with different cultures, races and beliefs. The process of assimilation generally elicits a very focused, site-specific response from the artist.

An early example of Kingerlee's sensitivity to the local scene is a group of nine miniature heads and figures, which he painted in 1977 during one of his visits to London (pp. 240-1). He had gone there from Cornwall in order to get some respite from the pressures of the domestic situation. The set up in London, however, was precarious, for he joined the urban squatters who had been in dispute with the Greater London Council for some time, only to finally negotiate an amnesty in 1977 that legitimised their status. Against this background the nine little pictures were painted onto used cardboard tickets from the London Underground. Writing some twenty-five years later, the artist explained the context for making these works:

> " the old London Transport Underground tickets … mark a time when I was living in a squat – Grafton Way, up the back of Warren St. station. … [I] was in a basement room and sometimes in the night in bed I could hear the trains far beneath in the Earth. A house of poor young musicians. So lots of music, day and night. 3 storey Georgian building. At the top a large grouping of gay people. Many of 'em now dead: Aids. The tickets themselves are antiques now. New technology ousted them. They're very charming little pieces of cardboard. "

These heads with their pallid, ghost-like features confront the viewer with a poignancy that belies their small scale. Each is a complete painting in its own right, while also functioning as part of a collective snapshot of a particular time and place.

In 1986 the artist spent three months in India. He was bowled over by the extraordinary colourfulness of the place – the smoke rising up from the cremations along the banks of the Ganges, the painted horns of the oxes and calves, and the tikka red dots on the brows of the Hindus. The experience was so different from what he was accustomed to in Ireland that he responded with a very distinct body of work. Temporarily abandoning pencil, ink and watercolour, he made a series of pastel drawings featuring figures, landscapes, heads and animals. A new lyricism was apparent in his use of radiant colours, which he speedily and confidently applied to pieces of buff-coloured paper. Not all the forms in these drawings are easy to read, but they generally comprise either a view with foreground and background, or else a composite scene incorporating a range of motifs and marks. One such work includes several heads, an Indian cow and a striped rug or piece of fabric, a seemingly odd assortment of things, and yet they are made to sit quite naturally on the page by virtue of the fluid lines and balanced composition.

For the last five or six years Kingerlee has been dividing his time between Ireland and Morocco, spending three months of every year in the ancient walled city of Fez (founded by Idris II, a direct descendant of Muhammad, in AD 808 as a royal residence and centre for religion,

Visit to India I
1986, pastel, ink on Indian paper, 14 cms x 18 cms

Visit to India II
1986, pastel, ink on Indian paper, 14 cms x 18 cms

science and law). He used to stay in an old part of the city but moved recently to a more modern district. Here he is surrounded by small children, which he finds very stimulating because of their quality of life, their infectious craziness and sense of fun. The people are poor, but they have great generosity of spirit and a sense of inner joyfulness. All of this impacts on his work, with the net result that it looks quite different from his Irish, Cornish, Indian and London series. Fez offers him a more complete – though still not total – escape from western influences than his exile in Beara is able to offer.

Trying to work in oil paints in Fez would simply not be practical, but he makes sure he is never without his notebooks and drawing materials. Hence the body of work inspired by the visits to Fez is restricted to works on paper. Some of these are drawn entirely in pencil outlines, quirky angular figures that emanate a Paul Klee-like lyricism (and with the same propensity for "taking a line for a walk", to quote the latter's famous dictum). Others are covered first with a fine network of lines, like a fishing net, on top of which the outline forms of men, women, children and animals are delicately superimposed. The pencil markings are sometimes smudged and blended with the finger, contributing to a sense of fragile beauty in the more realistic drawings. Other figures take on a wraith-like quality as a result of this treatment.

The artist's anarchic flouting of conventions, of rules of perspective and modelling for example, demands that these works are placed in an alternative context, a more vital tradition than that of western figuration. The art of so-called 'primitive' peoples might spring to mind, or alternatively of cave paintings, graffiti artists, or the unsullied vision of young children. Symbols familiar from graffiti and children's drawings are sometimes appropriated by Kingerlee, like the heart pierced by an arrow, a lemon-slice shape for a crescent moon, or a pointing arrow indicating the direction of someone's gaze.

One group of drawings explores a very specific Fez subject – that of a knife-grinder, whom the artist encountered in one of the narrow alleyways that link the various city gateways with the centre. The figure's posture, with one leg raised to pedal the grinding wheel whilst presenting a knife to its upper surface, proved to be a challenging one to draw. Rapid pencil sketches drawn on the spot captured the effort involved in the activity, but something was missing. Kingerlee was disappointed at not being able to represent the sparks that issued from the point of contact between metal and stone. Pondering this problem, he came up with an unusual idea: he would, quite literally, introduce fire into his drawings by burning holes in the paper with a red hot poker. In some of the drawings the holes are 'filled' from the back with postage stamps or other items of collage, but more commonly the visible surface of the paper is built up around the holes using a mixture of paint and sand. The resultant textures evoke the time-scarred, bill-posted and sometimes bullet-scarred walls of the old Moroccan city. When the accretions are formed into the shape of a head, however, the resultant effect can be disquieting (see *Knife-grinder of Fez I*, 2003). What began

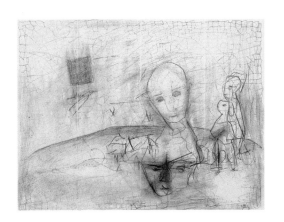

Italo Memory 3
2003, pencil on paper, 24 cms x 32 cms

Knife Grinder of Fez I
2003, oil and mixed media on paper, 15 cms x 20 cms

as a study of local life turns into something much more universal and timeless, an embodiment of a person imbued with pathos, empathy and a reminder that our bodies are but mortal shells. As the artist commented in a recent interview:

> " One of the best things we can do is think about our death, live today like we might not make it to the evening. Suddenly one gets a no messing quality – life's to be lived not to be wasted. "

CONCLUSION

HEADS, GOTHICS, Grids, Rub-backs, White-outs, Landscapes – the range and vitality of the work coming out of John Kingerlee's studio cannot fail to impress. Aged seventy, he is showing no signs of slowing down. On the contrary, his work regime would shame many an artist half his age. He is painting well and he knows it, but he is not the sort of man to shout it from the roof-tops. A private but knowing entry in his Journal of Work dated 15 July 2003 hints at an awareness of his place in the wider continuum of modern art:

> " At the beginning of the 20th Century: Cubism. The beginning of THIS Century: the Grids. Well, I wonder. Do you really think so? Perhaps. Just go on working. "

Kingerlee might also have cited James Joyce in his homage to early twentieth-century cultural trailblazers, for he esteems *Finnegan's Wake* as one of the greatest of novels. This is more than an act of reverence, however. At some level one cannot help but feel that the two men tap into the same wellspring of innovative creativity, accessible only to those who are willing to tear up the rule book and throw it away. Just as Joyce turned the novel on its head, questioning the very meaning of language and returning it to its pre-cognitive origins, so too has Kingerlee gone out of his way to reconfigure the grammar and meaning of painting. Through endless technical experimentation, trial and error, mixing and pouring, tearing, sticking and layering with brush and knife, he finally arrived in the early 1990s at a system of working that is virtually organic, whereby the picture evolves in three dimensions as well as the more traditional two. Indeed, it would not be an exaggeration to claim that his paintings are actually relief sculptures, so weighed down are they with the mass of accreted pigment.

Over periods often of years, the works in progress acquire ever greater richness and depth, not merely in pictorial terms, but also as highly nuanced and poetic statements. A by-product of the multi-layered surfaces is the necessary elision of self-contained forms and colours – the stripping away of the outward trappings of identity. Through the accumulated crusts and stipplings of oil paint we may well sense the presence of sea, sky, figures or animals, but the integrity of individual objects has been subordinated to an all-pervasive veil or atmospheric envelope. The sense of weightlessness and luminescence that is produced is the more amazing considering the density of what lies beneath. There is no place here for demonstrative gestures or expressively charged brushstrokes. Like stones thrown into ponds, they would serve only to break the stillness with their ripples.

Kingerlee intends that these profoundly meditative works should form a spiritual bastion against the ever-rising tide of materialism that is such a dominant force in our culture. The paintings may be modest in scale, but they are far from being modest in intention. One has to revert to Rothko to find a precedent for drawing a line so emphatically in the artistic sand.

KINGERLEE IN HIS OWN WORDS

On perception:

" Just to have an ocular anything is a miracle to start with. To see anything is a miracle. Just to be here is a miracle. I'd like to communicate that to people. Because I feel that more and more as this age progresses we are not having that sense of the miraculousness of being here. "

On passion:

" Art is a passionate thing for me and for many artists. "

On creativity:

" I rarely meet people as creative as me. I've met a few, but I hardly know what is meant by the word 'creativity'. Perhaps it's about possessing a heightened sensory awareness, which allows one to appreciate for example that the corner of the garden is lovely because that tree arches over, the grass is good and the boulder's just right to sit there. And one can enter into the landscape and the whole thing has got an extraordinary quality and feeling of its own. That would be creativity, wouldn't it, that's the way to live, isn't it? It comes from own's own feeling, one's own love. "

On experience:

" If you've been doing something for forty years you get good at it, you get very perceptive and quick at it, just by doing it. The brickie who's sixty and still at it is much better sussed than the brickie at sixteen who's just started, or the one at twenty. "

On chance:

" Sometimes you can get it wrong and another thing happens, and that thing can be good too. I love to work with what they call chance, cutting down on conscious choice, letting things arrive as they wish; keeping one's self out of it as much as possible by not making conscious choices.

Too much choice is an impoverishing situation. One's just there doing, and not fiddling about with choices too much. And then something arrives and a choice arises: will I keep it or will I destroy it? So all the way down the line there is choice, and no choice, and to get that right I do like to arrive at things energetically. "

On the gestural:

" I'm not as abandoned as Jackson Pollock, because there's a very slowed down, meditative sort of character lurking in me some of the time. The thing with Pollock is he was always violent, and I'm not violent like that. I am sometimes, because it's needed, but I get the feeling that Pollock was working with a ferocity that I'm not always working with. It's a fierce business swinging cans of paint around, moving fast. I can work and do work like that occasionally, but at the same time I love the way Braque would work, slowly and gently. So I'm operating to some extent in both those manners. "

On the unconscious:

" It's a weird word, the unconscious, because that's where the consciousness is. As Jung knew all his life, using the dreams to guide himself, it is the unconscious that knows everything, and truly our little consciousness is the one thing that doesn't matter. "

" When I'm painting I forget myself, I get lost. It's like meditation, and to forget oneself is wonderful. "

On the spiritual:

" I do like to get beyond mere conscious human endeavour into what you might call the 'gift' area – God will make it into something encharmed. People who work with dark forces let the devil and demonic entities enter the work. The human should turn to the light, be light, try and achieve the light. There's an aspect of the Reality that is pure light, and finally it ends up as this, what we experience as solid. "

On art and religion:

" I am forever mindful of the distinction between spirituality and culture – they are not one and the same thing! But if an authentic spirituality is the basis of culture, that's very wonderful. "

On titles:

" They can be deliberate, something someone says out of the blue, or a line of poetry or something mixed media. The titling I really like is what's given, what comes, in the same manner that the picture arrived.

I much prefer my own titles to those sometimes given later by other people. "

On life:

" The whole system is pushing us to a negative situation where we wonder whether life is worth living. People will kill themselves rather than go out and rob the bank. Don't kill yourself, go out and rob the bank. If you want to live go out and take chances, don't hurt people but go and do something desperate and begin to live like that. ... Now I'm older I can live closer to people, and with prayer I've got a greater understanding, but after a while if I'm amongst so-called normal people, I feel as if I'm going to go nutty, that people are beginning to live with so little passion or excitement or insanity, it's just so boring. "

On knowledge:

" Our noblest aspiration is for knowledge. We increase day by day in wisdom and knowledge that's useful. Have knowledge you can use. If it's useless, what is the point of it? The wisest people I know are the Sufis and therefore they are the best company. "

On recognition:

" I feel very happy, very grateful to the people who brought it and very grateful to the destiny that gave it to me. "

EXTRACTS FROM KINGERLEE'S JOURNAL OF WORK, 2003–04

Red Head in Field
2004, oil on canvas, 30 cms x 40 cms

Knife Grinder of Fez II
2003, collage and mixed media on paper,
20 cms x 16 cms

27 March 2003
Yesterday began blocking out areas on boards for Grid pictures. Finished two of these more than a year ago. CK has one, the other in Italy.

28 March
Burnt holes in Knife Grinder drawings with red hot poker at 10.30 tonight. Grid pictures drying above the stove. A day's drying above the stove is as good as a week's drying in the studio Mo reckons. Would Ezra Pound's *Cantos* be a good companion during the Grid paintings?

1 April
Brought in [to the house to dry] two Red Field heads. Both have two heads each. Sand and pigment in the heads. They're quite large. Start scribbling on pages of Trollope's novel *Rachel Ray*. Acid free paper.

3 April
Work on the Grids. New ones and two old ones. Slow work – many coats and oil takes so long to dry. Can it be speeded up? I wonder.

5 April
To Cork and back, bought materials. <u>Three primed canvases</u> a rare purchase. A twenty minute sprint around studio with palette knife – black, white, yellow ochre. One Field Head that had been oppressing changed to a freedom.

8 April
At kitchen table quickly marked with acrylic more than 60 large postcards Larry gave me to work on. Tom Carr and [Ana] Maria Pacheco p.c.s. Also at kitchen table put sand and P.V.A. mix into drawings of the Knife Grinder I saw in Morocco. Happy to have done this ….
In the studio Grids and the Head Field pictures. One of the Grids I've been working on for about three years is showing signs of coming to a conclusion.

9 April

… until lunch-time work on the Knife Grinder drawing: acrylic and emulsion onto the P.V.A. and sand. Seventeen of these on the go – all small works. Poker burns through Daler cartridge paper. Burnt holes backed by postage stamps. Colour glints.

18 April

Borrowed Con the framer's Grid painting. Great help: has clued me in on how to progress with the fourteen or more Grid pictures I'm involved with now.

First White Grid
2000, oil on canvas, 36 cms x 46 cms

21 April

… signed the little grey picture, a man, on the pigskin cardboard I took from a skip in Dublin years ago. Most of these pigskin cardboards are gone: a large number had the "Unstrung Heroes" on them.

28 April

This afternoon Grids in the studio. Coming on very slowly, as usual. Plonky plonk. Pokey poke … But later on a walk with Mo, away from the sea and then towards, the downhearted feeling about the Grids left me: Con's Grid came to mind and showed a way out towards finished pictures.

5 May

Work on kitchen table in afternoon mainly on Gerard's paper, around and sometimes across his rejected etchings. These papers vary in type from thin leathery paper to soft thick very absorbent paper. Have never had such a variety of paper to work with.

6 May

Thirteen pictures finished on Gerard's papers.

8 May

Early in the morning finish two paint-overs in the Lucian Freud book of his etchings. Hope to paint on all his etchings. Do it systematically from the first to the last. In studio – Grids. They begin to shape up. There are now twenty-four or more on the go. Also painted thin white on a couple of very textured old pictures, much reducing the colour and image that was there ….
Gone 11.00 pm now and there are seven pictures in the Freud etching book.

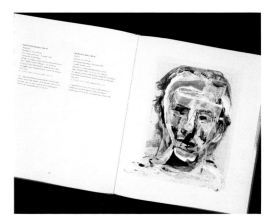

Head of a Man
paint-over in Lucian Freud etchings book

9 May

Two small heads into the house, on the postcard size cardboards (over 300 of them) which I bought in Dublin years ago. There must be over 200 of these cardboards left. Each of them is painted over with oil paint. Much drawn to doing a large number of abstracted very textured heads on them.

11 May

Mo drives us both up to Dublin. Do three or four Grid drawings in the travelling car – small sketchbook.

20 May

Mo out to yoga, me at kitchen table working on at 66 different paper surfaces with emulsions and acrylics. Began as black, white and grey but towards the end red and yellow crept in. An element of collage in many of them. Many of these surfaces are years old and began as drawings. Here and there Huguette's postage stamps stuck onto them. I have a large number of these stamps, from all over the world – although the most of them are Dutch. In the evening, mono-printed onto these surfaces a random white line of household emulsion.

27 May

Worked well at the postcard oils in the studio. They have been drying for about four days above kitchen stove.
Mixed up Red Lead with linseed oil, wore mask.

29 May

Any day I paint the Grids I read some of Ezra Pound's *Cantos* – a resolution.

1 June

In the morning signed and finished more than ten of the postcard sized oils. Bright, jewel-like. Much excited by them. It is pleasant painting oil on primed cardboard.

3 June

In the morning I added to the plaques of pigment on the Grid pictures, black mostly, it dries so swiftly and already these sections of colour begin to rise in isolation above the surface that surrounds them. As I see them completed in imagination, they are grey and white and off white, the bright and dark colours under-painted almost entirely vanished – but the small traces left adding to the power of the final surfaces. These pictures are in such contrast to the small oils which are so bright.

6 June

Went around all the Grid pictures and suddenly the possibility of completing them appears. They have begun to take on shape and colour. … This whole endeavour of the Grids thrills and delights me.

13 June

One small Grid into the house. Very spacious – the segments float in light and they are more of light than the light behind them … A DAY OF ABUNDANCE.

Time to Reflect
2003, oil on panel, 10 cms x 15 cms

1 July

Must explore the Grids: they seem to offer so much, despite their apparent poverty. Every time I think of Con's Grid (gone on loan to a show in Cork), I get a feeling of calm happiness. And what could be better in times like these?

6 July

… dug back through paint on a <u>large</u> canvas that had two heads on it. One of them looked like James Joyce. This is now hanging upside down above the kitchen sink, very wild, very lively and very unfinished. Won't rush it. Hang on: what needs to be done will reveal itself – all being well.

7 July

This afternoon worked mostly at the Grids with a spatulate brush and <u>not</u> a palette knife. Progress.

13 July

Yesterday was thrilled to see Con's Grid. Yes, I feel I can complete what I've begun, and more.

15 July

Perhaps all these Grids will begin to be finished together. They are there to be done. At the beginning of the 20th Century: Cubism. The beginning of THIS Century: the Grids. Well, I wonder. Do you really think so? Perhaps. Just go on working. Head down.

19 July

Most of the surfaces in the studio have been acquiring marks, or new surfaces entirely, for more than five years, often more than ten years. They are mostly boards. Amongst them are a few canvases. Suddenly after all these years they come to a swift, spontaneous conclusion. This is wonderful.

25 July, Dublin

Two visits to the Cobra show at Kilmainham [Irish Museum of Modern Art]. Enjoyed it very much. Cobra was a marvellous antidote to the darkness of World War Two in Europe. … how bright and playful the Cobraists must have seemed to those not outraged by them.

29 July

… the last of the Knife Grinder pictures leaves the house.

30 July

Hoorah! Have very nearly finished a medium sized Grid. It works all ways up. Need to live with it a while before final marks are made. It is good to be back at the Grids.

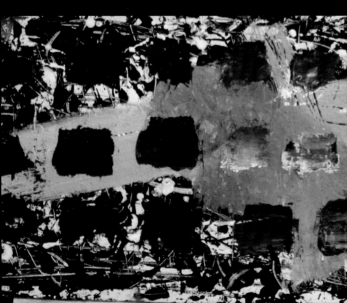

1 August
Finished four new paper works today. One of them an "Italo Picture."
It is 1.00 am. A good day's work.

2 August
Looked with Mo in a book this morning at some of Schwitter's collages
– reproductions of – how beautiful they are, and how far out they must
have been for most people in the '20s and '30s!

4 August
Two works on paper, acrylic, on the pages of Trollope's *American
Senator*. Acid free paper. No trace of the printed words left.

10 August
In the studio used up all the mounds of mixed colours. A strong red and
blue were predominant, so many boards, canvases and papers were left
darkened by the new paint.
Am longing to begin or rather return to the Grids. But tomorrow begins
the journey to Maroc.

11 August
Much taken by some small Cy Twomblys I've seen reproduced small.
Do his pictures need to be so big as they often are?

12 August
Flight from Cork to London, from London to Tangier. Arrived safely.
Drew at Heathrow while waiting. Youngsters peeped over my shoulder.
Very spontaneous marks.

20 August, Fez
Ten drawings done mostly in my local café. I have a solitary corner
where I can scribble away, literally, in peace. Rock n' Roll and African
Rap on the telly. Finished drawing on the ceramic floor of the cabina
with much water, rubbing back with an abrasive sort of washing up pad.
A good day's work!

29 August, Fez
Bought three camel hair brushes in La Ville Nouvelle some days ago.
"Made in China" it says on the exuberant red packaging but also
"Lefranc and Bourgeois, Fondé en 1720" which thrills me because of
the memory of the artist Patrick Hayman who once directed me to the
quality of Lefranc and Bourgeois's materials when I was visiting him at
his home in Barnes. …
The room in which I work here (at a small table, facing westish) has a
ceramic floor and the walls are tiled from the floor half way up to the
ceiling, which has coloured ornate carved plasterwork. The window is
to the north east. From it one sees Mount Zella and the passing trains.
The trains are close. When they go past the whole building judders

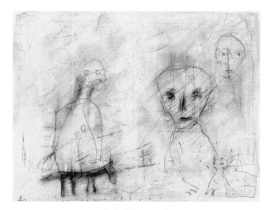

Italo Memory 2
2003, pencil on paper, 24 cms x 32 cms

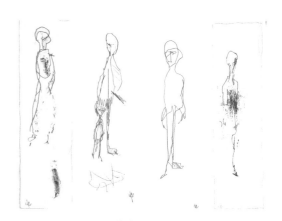

4 Walkabout Drawings
2005, pencil on paper, 28 cms x 9 cms

slightly. Also there is a large flat area where people walk to and fro, sit and converse and play football. Many in coloured robes, especially the women. Marvellous ….

Counted up this evening forty-seven works on paper finished since here in Fez. Many more papers to finish, they'll need emulsions, collage (especially the stamps Huguette gives me), mono-print. Anticipating this with pleasure.

2 September, Fez

Yesterday pleasure and inspiration from the long wall that runs past several different 'quartiers'. A light ochrous grey is the background to the various marks, signs, symbols and graffitis that adorn the wall. For me far more interesting than the blanket coverage of the Berlin Wall. There is one particular head painted in black with a very stubby brush, that is most inspiring. Yesterday made ten small heads thinking of this head on the wall. But my heads have too much personality in them (reminded me of Giacometti) – but this is not what I want: want the anonymity of the head on the wall – its sign-like quality – its letter-like quality – it does not have a 'this sort of a person' or a 'that sort of a person' quality.

5 September, Fez

Yesterday I found myself pleased that at the little table two foot something by three foot something, continually or rather very frequently surrounded by various tides of human life, friends, relatives, small children, gossip, laughter, arguments, the cassette player, further tides of Moroccan pop, sometimes Koran, the telly … I'm able to produce so much work. I do hope that this joyous, un-neurotic humanity which continually surrounds me enters the work, enriches it …

12 September, Fez

Yesterday was September 11 memorial day so, all day long on telly, images of the 'planes crashing into the New York skyscrapers and the buildings bursting into flames and then … collapsing on themselves in the way that an elevator descends. So many times in the movies immense destruction in New York, fictional of course, King Kong, Godzilla etc. but in no way did these fantasy images soften the power and violence of the images when they arrived in reality. Nothing on t.v. has gripped me like these images of the attack on the World Trade Centre buildings. My friend who is now a bishop wrote to me and asked would it enter into my work when the event first arrived. Well, I hope it will.

18 September, Fez

… have built up a pile of pictures … inspired by the wall. Did these pictures beginning in the morning after walking the length of the wall, looking at it the whole length of the walk.

September Eleven
2004, collage and mixed media on newsprint,
40 cms x 30 cms

22 October, Kilcatherine

At least a picture a day since the leaving of Morocco … Several double pages from Trollope's *American Senator* finished in acrylic and mounted, small oils on paper finished, abstracts, landscapes, two heads. One small, white and off white abstract landscape, much thrilled by, fulfilment of long, long-standing ambition. … Then the Grids, three of them almost complete – more than three! (Reaching the end of Ezra Pound's *Cantos*. Each Grid day has its *Canto*).

24 October

More bases of thick white onto board and canvas. Some black also, brief drawing. All from palette knife.

27 October

Have been mixing new colours, a red lead, a yellow ochre tinged with red, an ivory black, an earthy green and pile after pile of titanium white mixed up and used up. Many surfaces being built up in white and off white for the Whitey Abstract Landscapes. These flow forth easier and more abundantly than the Grids, for which am very grateful.

29 October

This day read the last of Ezra Pound's *Cantos*, and worked at the Grids. Will return to the first page and read with commentary.

30 October

In studio – Grids, and also more work at laying down grounds for "White Landscapes".

4 November

… have started extracting the colour from the stubs of coloured pencils. I split the wood of the stub with a knife, and crush the contents onto the paper I'm working on. Always enjoy doing this.
Grids are beginning to come together. A new White Landscape may be finished.

7 November

Long walk with Diba the dog, up the garden valley and down to the fingers where great handsome white waves crashed onto the rocks, and beyond that the Atlantic horizon – next stop New York (though to be more accurate I think it is Newfoundland!). Found mushrooms enough for a pan of soup. How late they are this year!

8 November

A lot of work with pencils onto the pages of *Rachel Ray* by Trollope in the evening – until late at night. Good results. A delight of working like this, here and there throughout the whole book, is that one does not know the final picture until the binding threads of the pages have been cut, for one cannot see the facing pages of each double sheet until the double sheets have all been removed from the book.

9 November

The Grids. A small one into the house – and as the leader of the band, the Grateful Dead said, after more than thirty years performing and travelling on the road – "I think we're getting the hang of it by now."

20 November

… mixed a red, a yellow ochre, a cadmium yellow and a zinc white. First time into studio since Belfast. Reworked a Grid I thought finished. It's back in the house again.

25 November

Friends visited today and loved the Grid paintings. Very pleased by this. Go on with them! In the past few days work has been mostly on paper at the kitchen table.

26 November

Long morning bath in which I began to read William Cookson's general introduction to each of Pound's *Cantos*. Exciting, exhilarating.
Late in the day began work on Grids – strong yellow, strong red going into them.

30 November

An exciting NEW sort of Grid into the house – much yellow in it. Mo slowed down my assault on this board, and then I began to see in it what she saw in it, I think, and it was far from what I was actually trying to achieve. I clung to this new vision and now I like this picture well. So thanks Mo.

10 April 2004

The Grids. The paint piles up on them, very deep now. So far these Grids are always hard to finish ….
Has been a good day for the paint stick rip stick pages. One puts the wet paint on the pages, closes the book, then later when the paint has dried or partially dried, one opens the book and the pages stick and rip, and then as one draws and marks the pages and repeats the process, the pages change and take on a singular and surprising liveliness. Usually several very interesting pages or rather pictures emerge from this process.

23 April

The Stick and Rip pictures are unique. Sometimes what is revealed is the centre of a page, not the back of a page, not the front of a page, but what is in between the two. It is a thrill to work on this new paper that has a woolly surface and which reveals in a misted way what is behind it. Now I go through the books painting and drawing on <u>both</u> sides of the pages. Sometimes those tiny gems, postage stamps get stuck in and also much old collage material is used …

Grid Composition Yellow
2004, oil on board, 46 cms x 50 cms

Stick and Rip
2004, collage and mixed media on book pages,
20 cms x 24 cms

17 May, Granada

… much work at the kitchen sink on small sketchbook pages, rubbing back under running water, sometimes washing page with soapy finger. Pencils and black watercolour pencil. A large number done and Mo really likes at least eight of them. They are all in the Taschen *Bauhaus* book flattening out, because the pages get very wavy with all the rubbing and water absorption and the drying at the electric heater.

31 May, Kilcatherine

Back from Granada for over a week … The camera came into the studio and I was filmed working. I'm told it's to go out on *Nationwide* on the telly in a few weeks' time. I do not enjoy myself being seen by a very large number of people, but I do enjoy the prospect of the actual oil paintings being seen on national television.

16 June

The oils on the postcard sized cardboards are coming to an end. Over twelve years ago in Dublin those pieces of cardboard were bought. Not sure how many – very likely more than 300 pieces. And now less than fifty to be finished. These later ones have become very bright, thick, chunky oils. Much pleased by them and so are other people.

The Show Off
2002, oil on board, 18 cms x 25 cms

20 June

As soon as a picture is finished in the studio I hasten into the house with it whether it is large or very small, for each removal is a lessening of the din of surfaces crying out "please finish me, please finish me!"

21 June

Drawings like *Finnegan's Wake*: one image hides another, one image hides another. That face is a face that becomes a mountain, that nose becomes a figure in a djellaba, that eyebrow is a fish and so on.

2 September, Fez

Working hard in uncomfortable circumstances – no table, perched on bed's edge, somewhat the prey of two very small children – am pleased by how much I've done, although what I have done comes nowhere near what I wish for. The eroded abstraction, the free of the ego's will wished for has not yet arrived: always the little dancing figures and all their creatures and animals want to get into the picture, which frequently they do. Am not overly ruthless about excluding them, but will try to be so this day.

7 September, Fez

Yesterday not a finished picture, but perhaps four pages worth keeping for later work in Ireland. <u>Remember the visions of those pictures that came when the money was gone!</u> How clear and strong the white – WHITES – were!

Stick and Rip
2004, collage and mixed media on book pages,
22 cms x 32 cms

12 September, Fez

The "Rip Ups" have been the adventure of this Maroc visit. They still are. Few of them are actually finished – they need sticking down and then some work on them. Only a vague idea what work.

14 September, Fez

Two rather crowded drawings – pleased with them. Crowded like the crowd behind the newly circumcised little boy being carried on his litter cum throne head high. Deep sounding drums, great slender trumpets six or seven feet long. It passed by the café the other day. These drawings are the mosaics blown apart. Did them on the bed. A difficult day.

24 September, Fez

Vigorous work with coloured pencils on twenty-five different sheets of paper … From one sheet to the next very swiftly … These works spontaneous, joyful, wild. Doing them certainly cheers me up even when the gloomy doomies are very strong within.

29 September, Fez

Used the bath for scrubbing back and overall staining from the watercolour pencil marks, which flow forth their colours abundantly when wetted. These flowing colours are mostly reds and oranges. Also there is a brilliant yellow that gushes forth across the page, or paper.

12 October, Kilcatherine

Morning worked oils studio. Afternoon in kitchen black and white emulsions onto at least thirty-one of the drawings done in Fez.

21 October

Mo was not enthused by the work from Fez. Well, I can do further work on them, and there were at least twenty good pieces. It is the figures she doesn't like – wants me to be more abstract. And I do as well, but the figures – in the paper work – insist on creeping in. Perhaps I must close the door on them more firmly.

25 November

A day in Cork. Two oils into the Crawford [Municipal Art Gallery] for a Cork artists' show. Abundance of whitish chewing gum spit-outs flattened and sticking to the pavements – like little lichens in the middle of the city.

Early Works

Lovers
1962, oil on board, 36 cms x 48 cms

Sheep in Snow
1962, oil on board, 18 cms x 36 cms

Heron, Warwickshire
1962, oil on board, 38 cms x 61 cms

Horse Head
1967, painted collage, 38 cms x 26 cms

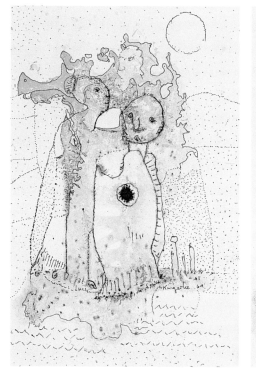 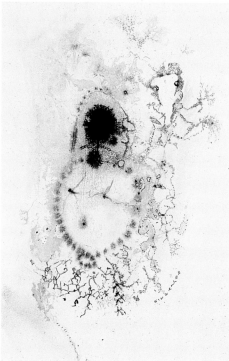 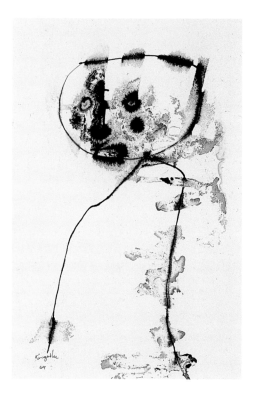

Hash Drawings
1969, ink on paper, 16 cms x 10 cms

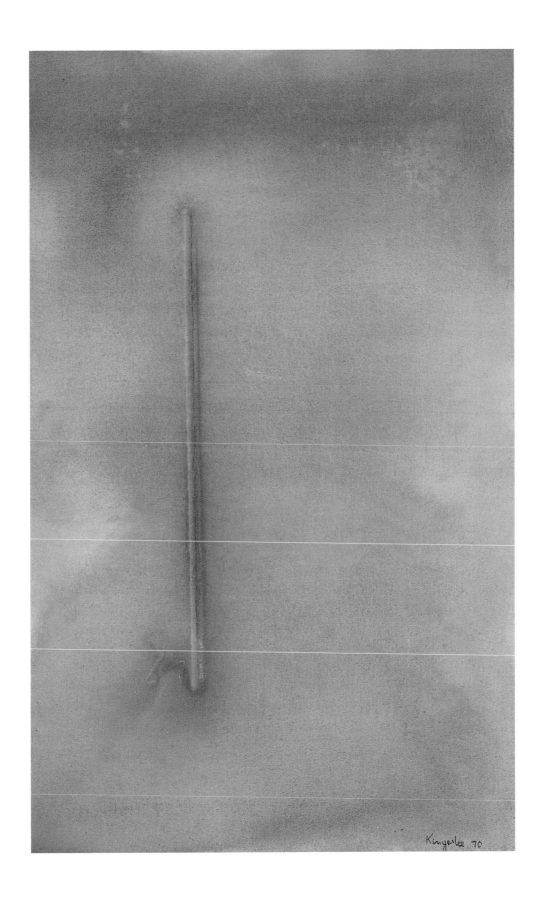

Zip Painting, Cornwall
1970, acrylic on calico, 84 cms x 53 cms

Ibiza
1969/70, pen and ink on paper, 46 cms x 22 cms

Birds in Space
1972, pen and ink on paper, 38 cms x 28 cms

Painted Collage
1977, collage on board, 52 cms x 62 cms

Observations
1977, pen and ink on paper, 20 cms x 12 cms

A Walk in the Park
1983, oil on canvas, 43 cms x 29 cms

Landscapes and Figures

The Pilgrim Forsakes the Magician
1979, oil on canvas, 66 cms x 90 cms

Lingam (Just the Whisper)
1986, oil on canvas, 66 cms x 92 cms

Coming to the Man in Tree
1989, oil on canvas, 47 cms x 60 cms

Whirling Figure
1990, oil on board, 50 cms x 30 cms

View from a Window
1990, oil on board, 25 cms x 20 cms

Autumn Wanderers
1990, oil on canvas, 30 cms x 50 cms

Still Life
1990, oil on canvas, 30 cms x 40 cms

Landscape
1991, oil on canvas, 46 cms x 67 cms

Still Life
1992, oil on canvas, 50 cms x 60 cms

Prisoner with a Clue
1992, oil on board, 27 cms x 24 cms

Landscape
1992, oil on board, 33 cms x 41 cms

Waterside Reflection
1992, oil on canvas, 30 cms x 25 cms

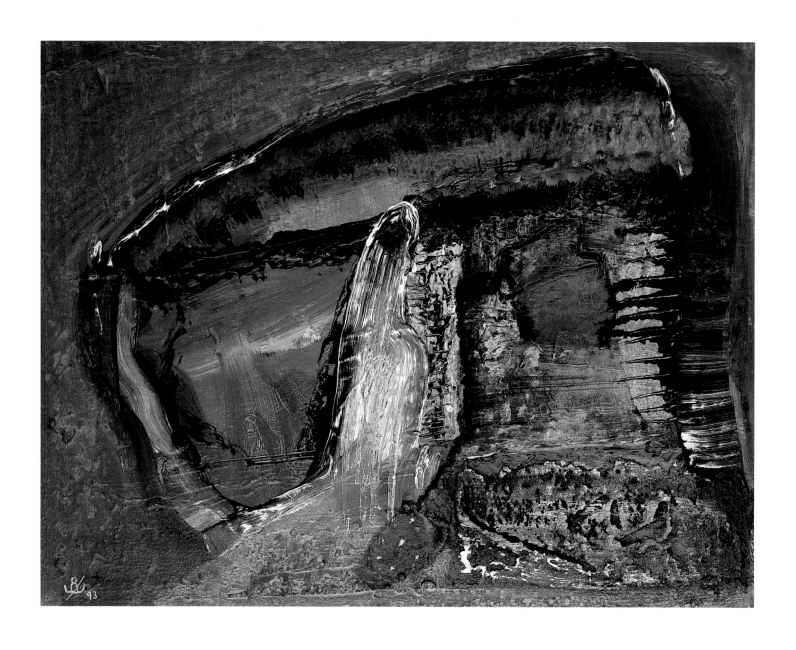

Landscape with Standing Stone
1993, oil on board, 34 cms x 44.5 cms

Three Figures and Bird
1994, oil on paper, 35 cms x 25 cms

Kilcatherine Landscape
1994, oil on board, 18 cms x 36 cms

Landscape Composition
1994, oil on board, 15 cms x 13 cms

The Bed, The Bird, The Butterfly
1994, oil on canvas, 36 cms x 68 cms

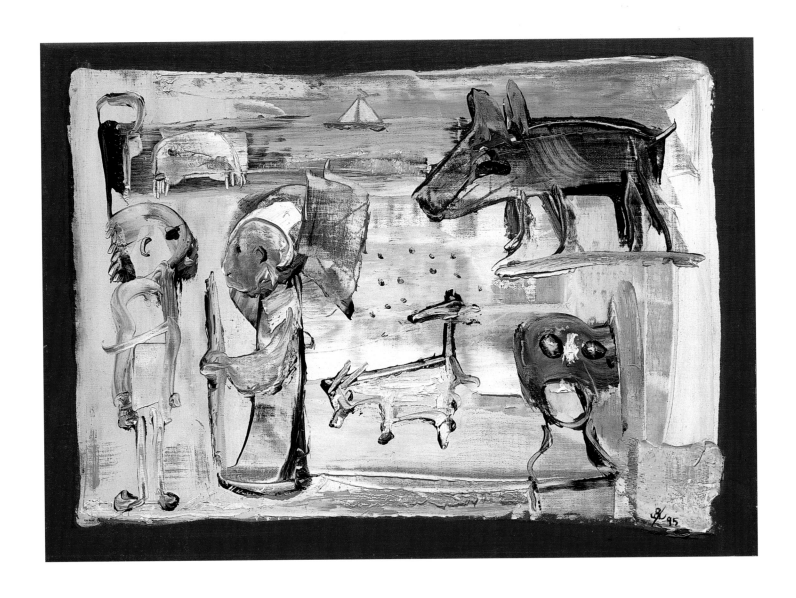

An Historic Moment
1995, oil on canvas, 14 cms x 20 cms

Morocco
1996, oil on canvas, 44 cms x 38 cms

Multitude
1996, oil on canvas, 71 cms x 122 cms

The Warrior
1996, oil on paper, 22 cms x 30 cms

The Guardian of Beara
2000–04, oil on board, 28 cms x 46 cms

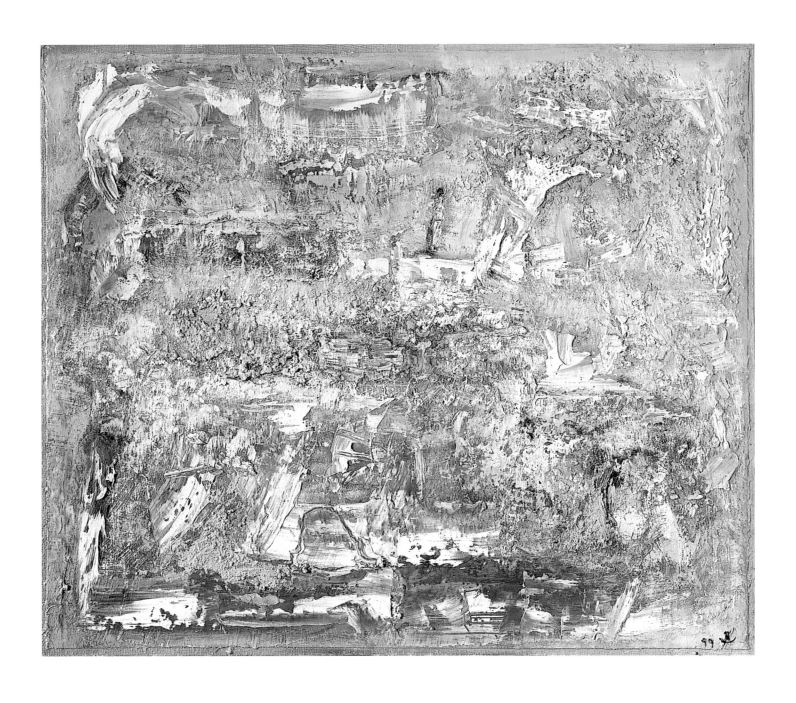

Merrily Into the Wilderness
1999, oil on board, 51 cms x 61 cms

Assembly and Fish
1999, oil on canvas, 36 cms x 46 cms

Birdsong
1999, oil on canvas, 18 cms x 24 cms

The Blue Beyond
2001, oil on board, 18 cms x 58 cms

Birds and the Kingdom
2002, oil on canvas, 37 cms x 43 cms

Mabinogian
2002, oil on board, 40 cms x 65 cms

Beara Landscape
2002, oil on board, 18 cms x 28 cms

The Show Off
2002, oil on board, 18 cms x 25 cms

Exercise Time
2002, oil on board, 10 cms x 15 cms (actual size)

Homage to Beara
2003, oil on board, 15 cms x 23 cms

Landscape
2003, oil on canvas, 18 cms x 24 cms

Figures on the Shore
2003, oil on board, 28 cms x 38 cms

The Chase
2003, oil on canvas, 20 cms x 28 cms

The Rich Landscape
1995–2003, oil on board, 36 cms x 48 cms

Heads and Fields II
2003, oil on canvas, 40 cms x 58 cms

Heads and Fields III
2003, oil on canvas, 40 cms x 50 cms

Heads and Fields IV
2003, oil on canvas, 44 cms x 60 cms

Busy Day in Beara
2003, oil on board, 10 cms x 15 cms (actual size)

Passing by Unnoticed by Some
2003, oil on board, 10 cms x 15 cms (actual size)

Viewpoint
2003, oil on board, 10 cms x 15 cms (actual size)

The Preacher Man
2003, oil on board, 15 cms x 10 cms (actual size)

Time to Reflect
2003, oil on board, 10 cms x 15 cms (actual size)

Seascape
2003, oil on board, 10 cms x 15 cms (actual size)

The Wanderer
2003, oil on board, 10 cms x 15 cms (actual size)

Looking Towards Kilcatherine
2004, oil on board, 19 cms x 29 cms

The Dogman's Story
2004, oil on canvas, 16 cms x 26 cms

A Boat's in the Tree Day
1996–2004, oil on canvas, 50 cms x 75 cms

Glory
2004, oil on board, 16 cms x 20 cms

A Group of Admirers
2004, oil on board, 22 cms x 34 cms

Timeless Memory
2004, acrylic on card, 36 cms x 26 cms

Animal Kingdom
2004, oil on board, 30 cms x 40 cms

Village and Lake
2004, oil on canvas, 29 cms x 40 cms

Yellow Dog in Landscape
2004, oil on canvas, 36 cms x 40 cms

A Stroll in Kilcatherine
2004, oil on canvas, 15 cms x 25 cms

Ballycravorn
1991–2004, oil on canvas, 46 cms x 66 cms

Shoreline
1995–2004, oil on board, 30 cms x 52 cms

Beautiful Kilcatherine
1995–2004, oil on board, 29 cms x 59 cms

Peeks
1999–2004, oil on card, 21 cms x 26 cms

The Encounter
1994–2004, oil on board, 30 cms x 42 cms

Looking Out to Sea
2003, oil on board, 17 cms x 23 cms

Kilcatherine
1997–2004, oil on board, 29 cms x 39 cms

Figures in Landscape
2000–2004, oil on board, 28 cms x 20 cms

People Walking Through Landscape
2001–2004, oil on board, 24 cms x 16 cms

Walk on By
2000–2004, oil on canvas, 29 cms x 25 cms

The Gathering on Beara
2000–04, oil on canvas, 30 cms x 30 cms

Landscape
2004, oil on canvas, 25 cms x 32 cms

Hope Springs Eternal
2004, oil and mixed media on board, 25 cms x 35 cms

Gothic
2004, acrylic on card, 22 cms x 33 cms

Celebrate the Purity of Nature
2001–2004, oil on board, 21 cms x 30 cms

Gothic
2004, acrylic on board, 31 cms x 59 cms

Landscape
2005, oil on board, 26 cms x 50 cms

White Landscape Composition
2005, oil on board, 32 cms x 40 cms

Passing Through
2005, oil on board, 25 cms x 30 cms

Beara Landscape
2005, oil on board, 25 cms x 40 cms

Passing Through Kilcatherine
1998–2005, oil on board, 31 cms x 47 cms

The Journey is Finished
1979–2005, oil on canvas, 28 cms x 40 cms

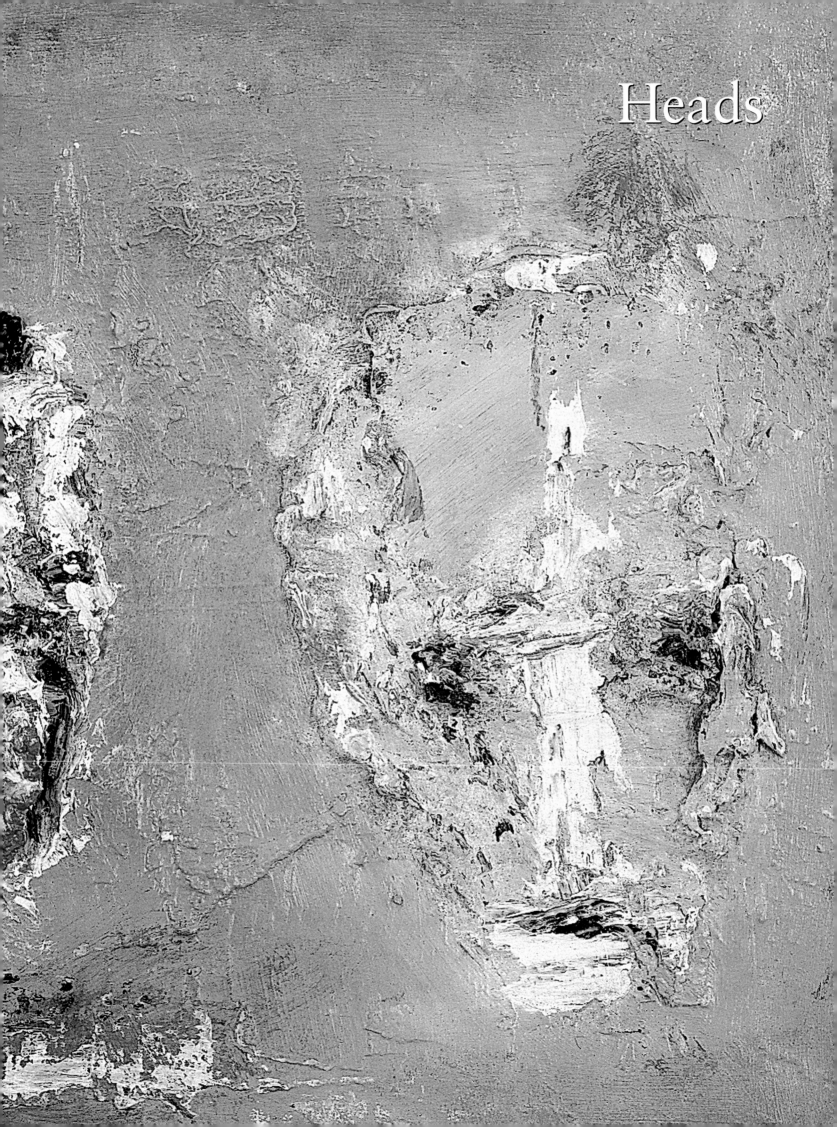

The Holy Man
1980, oil on board, 22 cms x 18 cms

Head
1983, oil on card, 20 cms x 10 cms

Birdman
1986, oil on board, 30 cms x 20 cms

Head (Cleanagh)
1987, acrylic on canvas, 51 cms x 41 cms

Bird Overhead
1995, oil and mixed media on paper, 24 cms x 15 cms

Heads in Landscape
1997, oil on paper, 28 cms x 20 cms

Profiles
1999, oil on card, 23 cms x 18 cms

Lost in Time
2002, oil on board, 26 cms x 19 cms

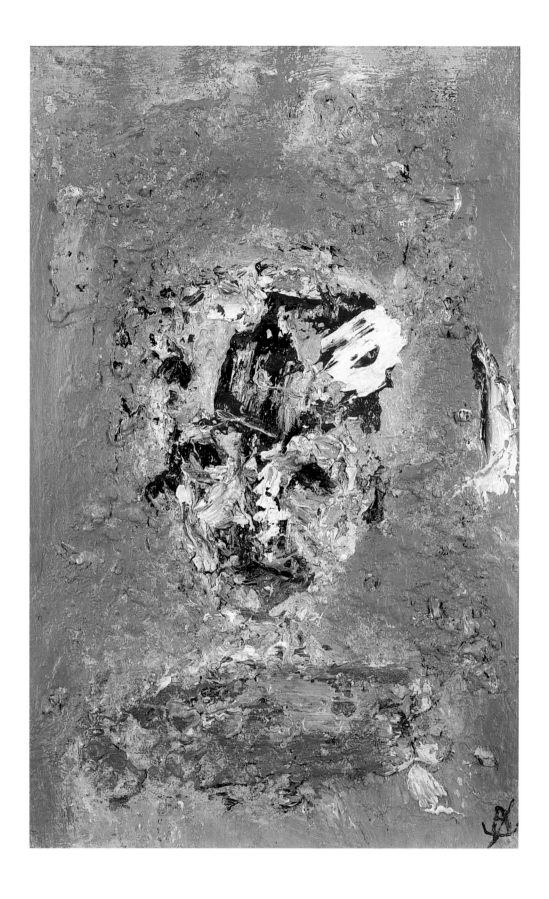

Head
2002, oil on board, 25 cms x 15 cms

Solitary Man
2002, oil on board, 23 cms x 15 cms

Three Heads
2002, oil on canvas, 30 cms x 50 cms

Head
2002, oil on board, 30 cms x 20 cms

Head in Landscape
2002, oil on board, 25 cms x 20 cms

Head
2003, oil on canvas, 28 cms x 18 cms

The Local
2003, oil on board, 28 cms x 18 cms

Head
2003, oil on board, 27 cms x 17 cms

The Witness
2003, oil on board, 26 cms x 18 cms

Head in Landscape
2000–2003, oil on card, 24 cms x 18 cms

Three Heads I
2003, oil on canvas, 10 cms x 25 cms

Three Heads II
2003, oil on canvas, 10 cms x 25 cms

The Line-up
2003, oil on board, 20 cms x 40 cms

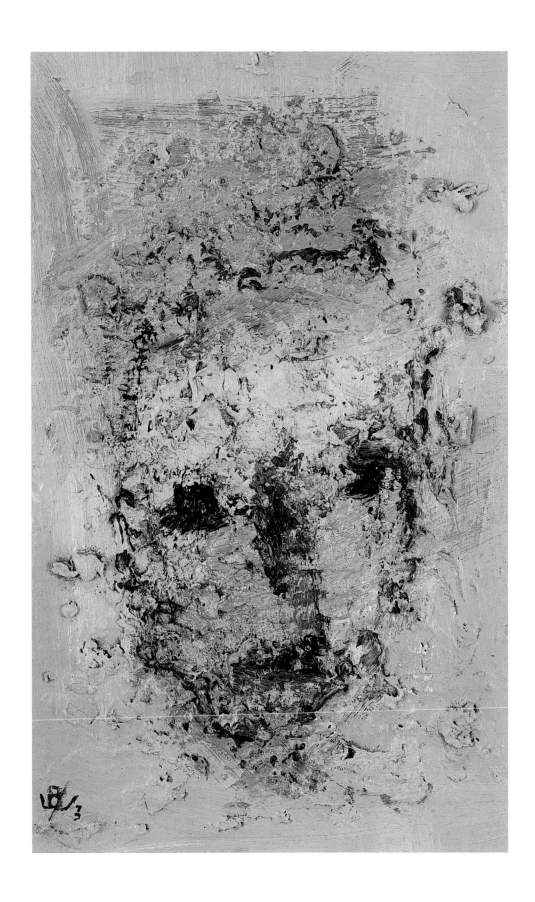

Head
2003, oil on board, 25 cms x 15 cms

Head
2003, oil on board, 23 cms x 15 cms

Head
2004, oil on board, 25 cms x 17 cms

Red Head in Field
2004, oil on canvas, 30 cms x 40 cms

Many Faces
2001–2004, oil on board, 20 cms x 28 cms

Conversation
2004, oil on board, 20 cms x 20 cms

Passing Through
2004, oil on board, 20 cms x 24 cms

Set Me Free
2004, oil on board, 24 cms x 34 cms

Tête-à-Tête
2004, oil on board, 15 cms x 10 cms (actual size)

Grids

Beara Landscape
1996, oil on canvas, 36 cms x 44 cms

Early Grid Painting
1997, oil on board, 23 cms x 15 cms

Early Grid Painting
1998, oil on board, 20 cms x 28 cms

First White Grid
2000, oil on canvas, 36 cms x 46 cms

Grid of Life
2003, oil on board, 25 cms x 37 cms

Wall in Fez
2003, oil on board, 34 cms x 50 cms

Grid Composition
2003, oil on paper, 30 cms x 20 cms

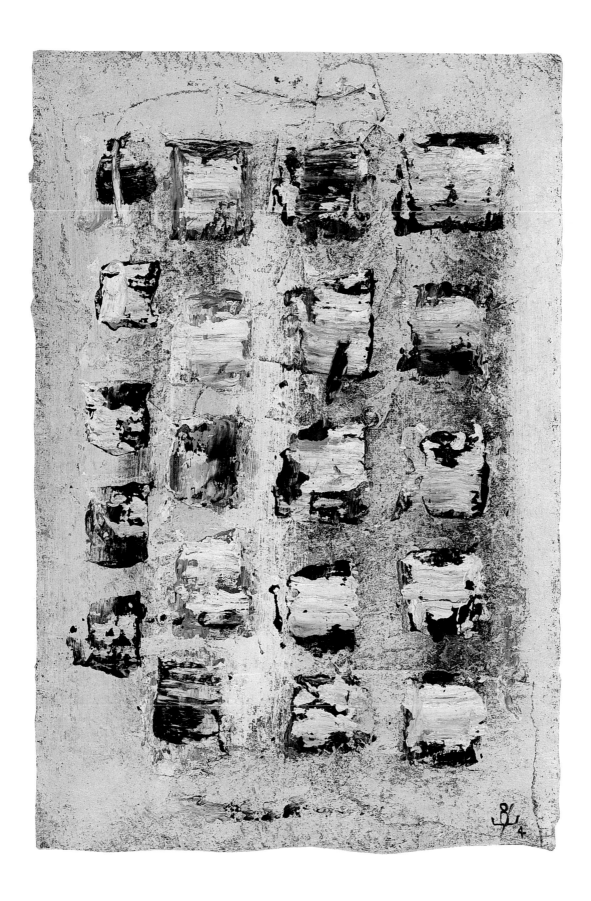

Grid Composition
2004, oil on paper, 28 cms x 19 cms

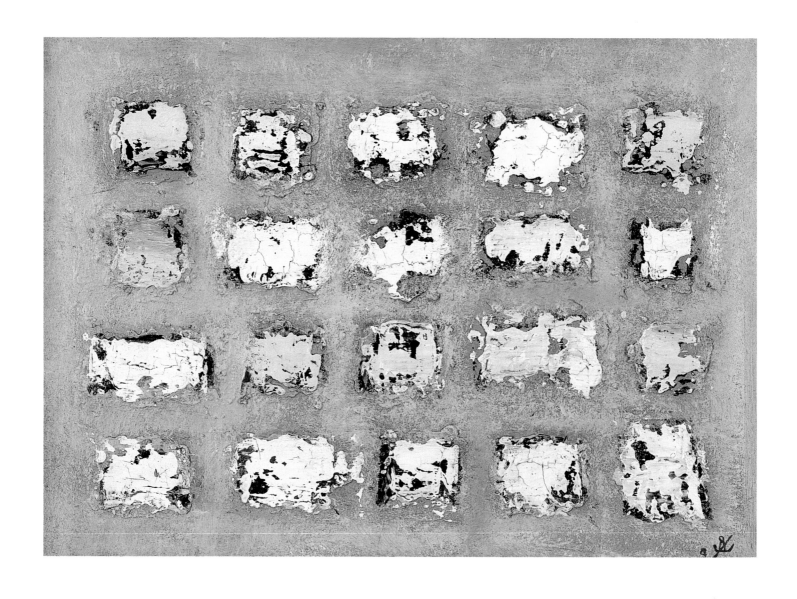

Grid Composition
2000–2004, oil on board, 21 cms x 31 cms

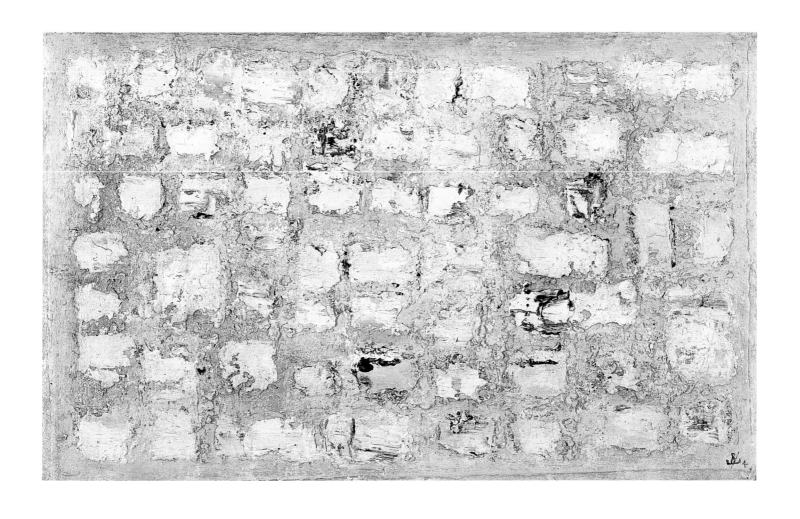

Grid Composition
1997–2004, oil on board, 32 cms x 52 cms

Grid Composition Yellow
2004, oil on board, 46 cms x 50 cms

Blue Grid I
2004, oil on board, 19 cms x 28 cms

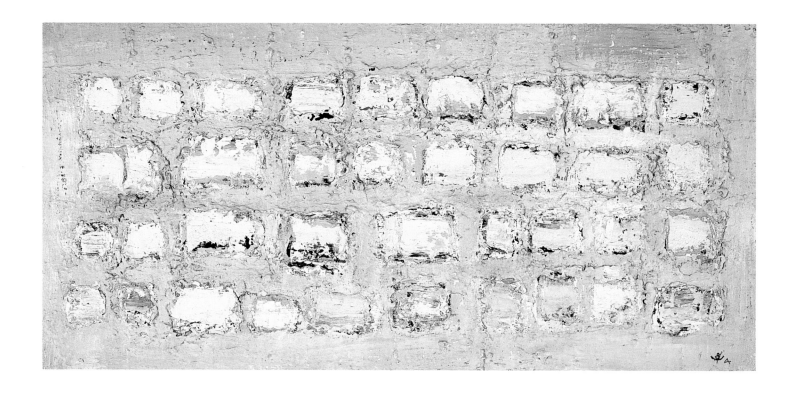

Grid Painting
2004, oil on board, 28 cms x 59 cms

Grid Composition
1998–2004, oil on board, 30 cms x 53 cms

Grid Composition
2000–2004,
oil on board,
30 cms x 53 cms

Grid Composition
2000–2004, oil on board, 31 cms x 27 cms

Grid Composition
2000–2004, oil on board, 19 cms x 30 cms

Blue Grid II
2004, oil on paper, 19 cms x 28 cms

Grid Composition
1998–2004, oil on board, 29 cms x 41 cms

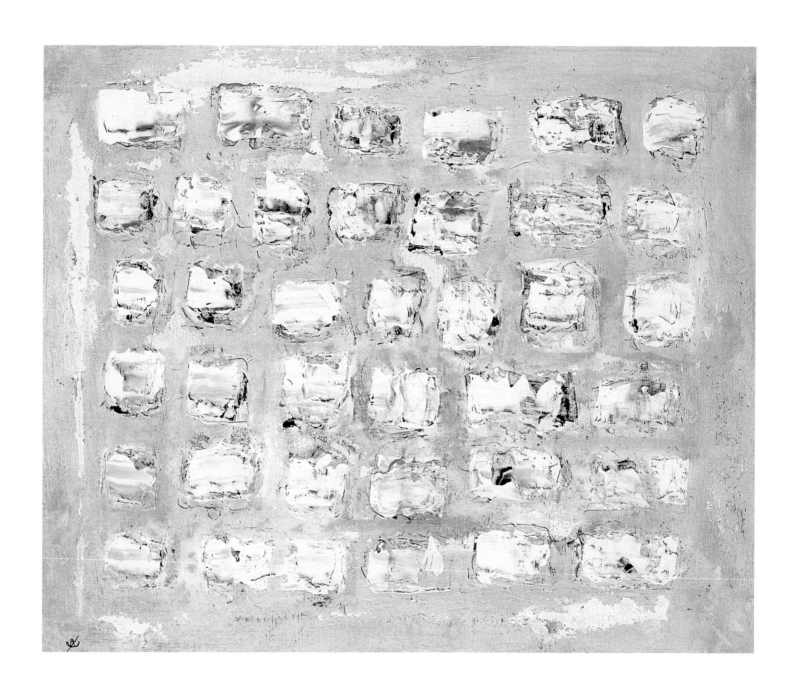

Grid in Granada I
2005, acrylic on canvas, 32 cms x 40 cms

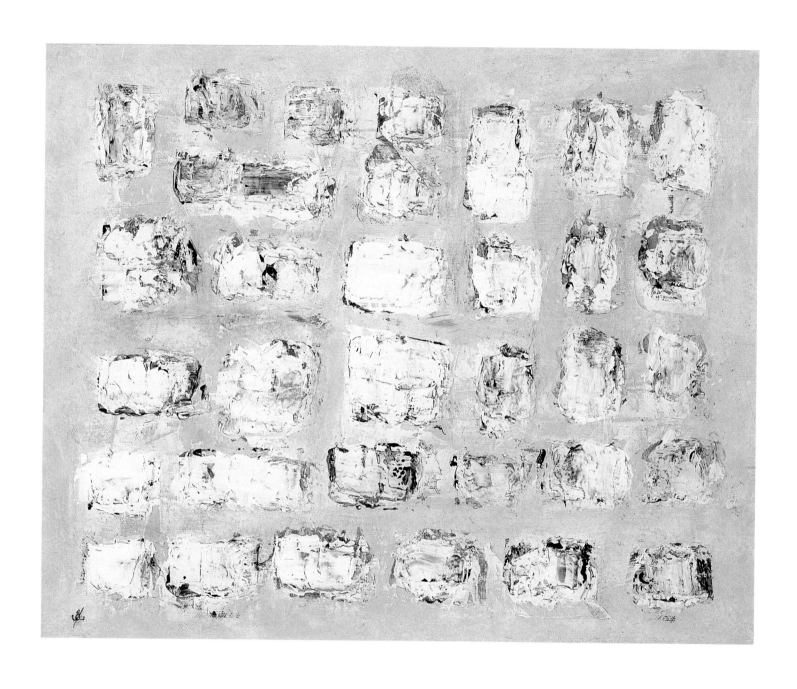

Grid in Granada II
2005, acrylic on canvas, 32 cms x 40 cms

Grid in Granada III
2005, acrylic on canvas, 40 cms x 32 cms

Grid in Granada IV
2005, acrylic on canvas, 52 cms x 40 cms

Grid in Granada V
2005, acrylic on canvas, 50 cms x 40 cms

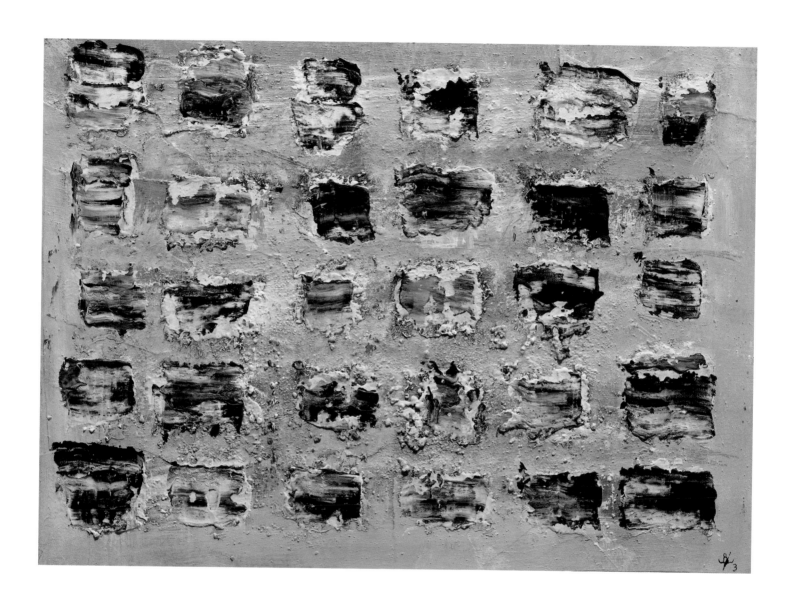

Grid Composition
2003, oil on board, 32 cms x 43 cms

Grid Composition
1997–2004, acrylic on board, 29 cms x 41 cms

Rub-Backs

Tribute One
2001, acrylic on board, 25 cms x 17 cms

Tribute Two
2001, acrylic on board, 25 cms x 17 cms

Tribute Three
2001, acrylic on board, 14 cms x 19 cms

Tribute Four
2001, acrylic on board, 14 cms x 19 cms

Tribute Five
2002, acrylic on paper, 20 cms x 27 cms

Tribute Six
2002, acrylic on board, 27 cms x 20 cms

Collages and Works on Paper

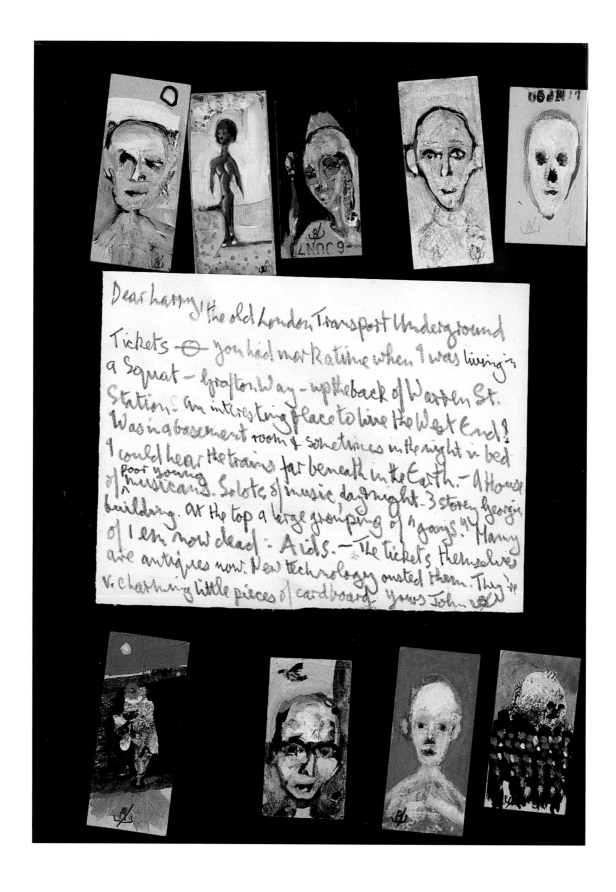

Nine London Underground Tickets, Grafton Way
1977, mixed media on card

Nine London Underground Tickets, Grafton Way (reverse)
1977, mixed media on card

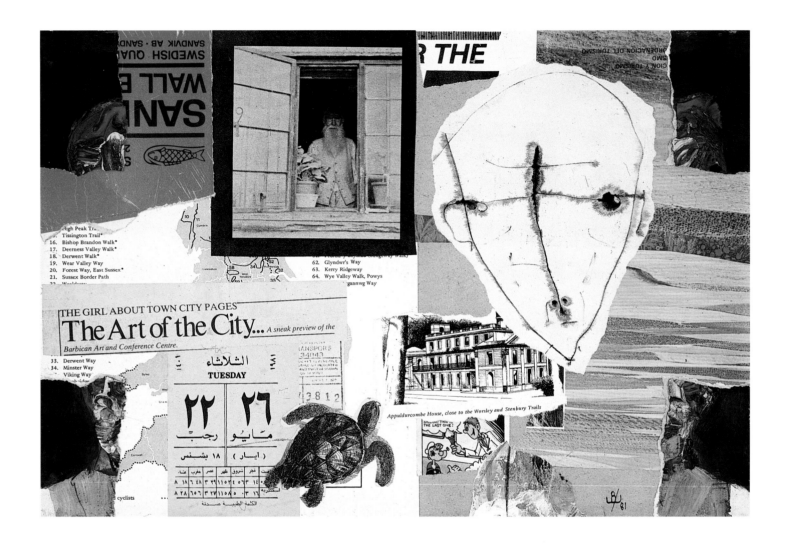

Art of the City
1981, collage and mixed media on card, 25 cms x 37 cms

The Kerry Circus
1982, collage and mixed media on board, 45 cms x 30 cms

Ears Have Walls
1990, mixed media on paper, 12 cms x 15 cms

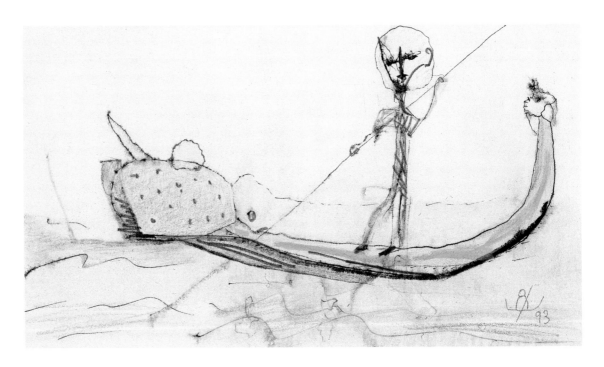

Paddling My Own Canoe
1993, mixed media on paper, 10 cms x 17 cms

The Fish Man
1995, mixed media on card, 25 cms x 15 cms

Titanic
1995, collage and mixed media on card, 16 cms x 24 cms

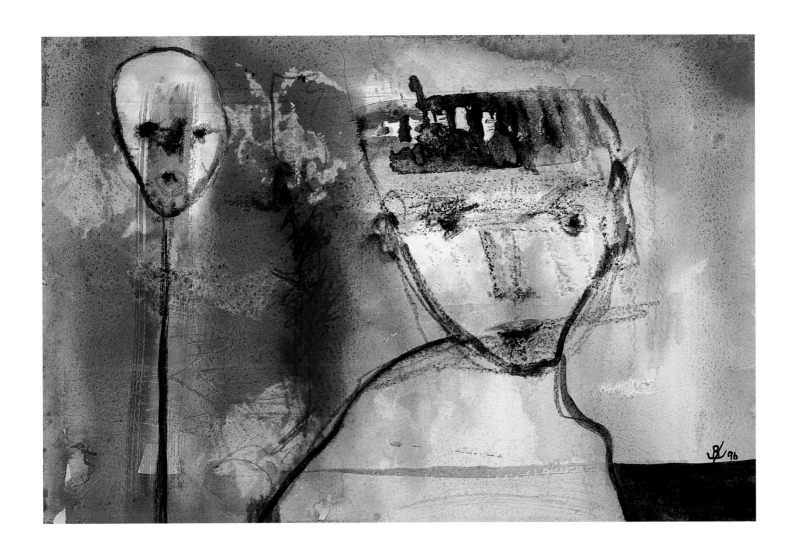

Living the Past
1996, mixed media on paper, 38 cms x 58 cms

The Swimmer
1997, watercolour and mixed media on paper, 15 cms x 23 cms

Commuting
1997, collage and mixed media on paper, 20 cms x 30 cms

End of Discussion
1999, collage and mixed media on paper, 30 cms x 22 cms

Circle
2000, mixed media on book pages, 15 cms x 23 cms

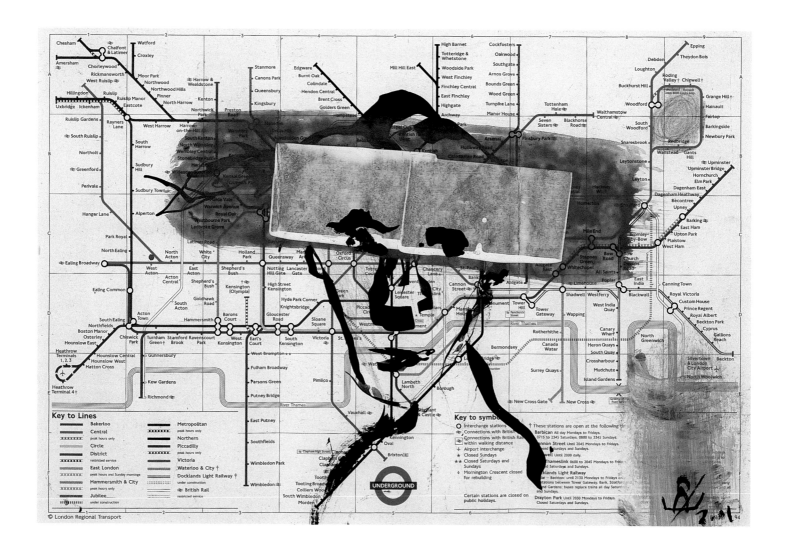

Underground
2001, collage and mixed media on London Underground map, 14 cms x 18 cms

Eloquence
2001, watercolour and mixed media on paper, 12 cms x 10 cms

Early Days All Days
2003, collage and mixed media on paper, 24 cms x 35 cms

Preying for Time
1989–2003, oil and mixed media on paper, 22 cms x 21 cms

Shocking News
2003, collage and mixed media on paper, 20 cms x 26 cms

Walking the Dog
2003, mixed media with sand on paper, 15 cms x 20 cms

Knife Grinder of Fez I
2003, oil and mixed media on paper, 15 cms x 20 cms

Knife Grinder of Fez II
2003, collage and mixed media on paper, 20 cms x 16 cms

Sotheby's Series
2003, collage and mixed media on printed paper, 24 cms x 17 cms

Butcher's Bill
2003, collage on paper, 20 cms x 16 cms

Cinematic
2003, mixed media with sand on paper, 15 cms x 20 cms

Photographic Memories
2004, collage and mixed media on Indian paper, 18 cms x 27 cms

The Journey
1999–2004, collage and mixed media on paper, 24 cms x 17 cms

September Eleven
2004, collage and mixed media on newsprint, 40 cms x 30 cms

Ship and Shore
2004, collage and mixed media on paper, 21 cms x 29 cms

Affairs to Remember
2004, collage and mixed media, oil and sand on paper, 21 cms x 25 cms

Inside Out
2004, collage and mixed media on paper, 29 cms x 20 cms

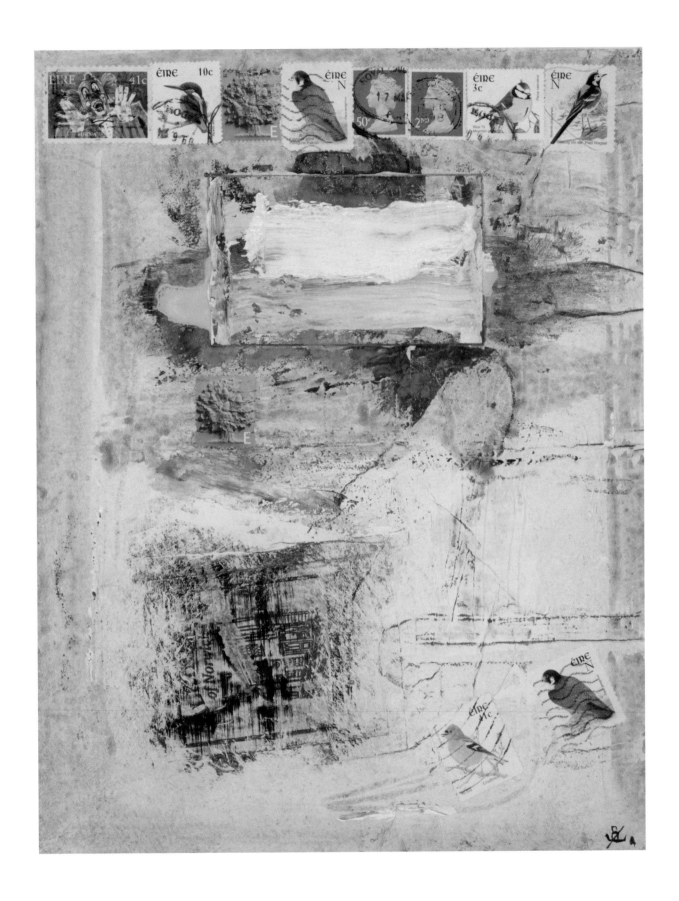

In Memory of the Tea Shop Man
2004, collage and mixed media on paper, 27 cms x 21 cms

Imagery One
2005, collage and mixed media on paper, 30 cms x 23 cms

Imagery Two
2005, collage and mixed media on paper, 30 cms x 23 cms

Self Portrait Paint-over
2005, acrylic on photograph, 25 cms x 20 cms

Walking Through
2005, painted collage on board, 30 cms x 24 cms

Imagery Three
2005, collage and mixed media on paper, 23 cms x 30 cms

CHRONOLOGY

1936

17 February, born in Birmingham; moves to London aged six weeks

1939

Moved to 32 Clifton Road, Paignton

1949–55

Attended St Mary' School, Winslade Park, Clyst St Mary as a boarder

1955

Worked for BSA or Raleigh bikes in Aston

1956

Looked after the gardens at special needs school Kenbury House, Kenbury

1957

Spent a year in Soho

1958

Married, moved to Islington and worked on a building site

1959–60

Worked for the Camphill Village Trust at Botton Hall, Danby Dale, near Whitby

1960

Worked at Newnham-on-Severn branch of the Camphill Village Trust

Managed an organic flour mill at Hunsingore near Wetherby

1961

Worked in an organic market garden at Hockley Heath, Umberslade, Warwickshire

1962

Moved to cottage at Trevarrick near Mevagissey, Cornwall

1965

Death of father; moved to cottage at Treveor near Gorran, Cornwall

1967

10 March – 6 April, first solo show, comprising 41 works in cryla, PVA, collage, oil and drawings, Ewan Philips Gallery, Maddox Street, London

1968

Until 21 February, exhibition of paintings, drawings and collages, Foxhole School Exhibition Room, Dartington College, Dartington

4 – 29 September, exhibition of 43 paintings, 13 drawings and 7 cryla, Walton Gallery, 162 Walton Street, London SW3 (the catalogue contains an essay on primitive art by Sheldon Williams and a preface by Sir Anthony Cooper)

1969

Spent a year in Ibiza and made his first visit to Morocco

1972

3 July – 11 August, participated in Summer Exhibition, Prudhoe Gallery, 79 Duke Street, Grosvenor Square, London

1975

Worked for potter Jeff Savage for a year at The Salt Box, Ennis Cavern, St Dennis, Cornwall

Started own pottery in cottage at Treveor, marking the pots with a stamp of a man in a boat, a motif he had also begun to apply to paintings

1976

Death of mother, Violet Mary Wedgwood Kingerlee, 104 Preston Down Road, Paignton

1977

Lived in 'squat' in Grafton Way at the back of Warren Street tube station, London

1 – 19 November, exhibition of 20 works, Drian Galleries, 7 Porchester Place, London W2 2BT

1979

Worked in the basement of a house in Bath for several months

1981

Walking holiday going round the Dingle Peninsula, County Kerry

1982

October, moved to remote cottage at Cleanagh near Allihies, Beara Peninsula, West Cork (the cottage and its setting featured in the BBC's 1998 dramatisation of Deirdre Purcell's novel *Falling for a Dancer*, set in 1930s West Cork).

1986–87

Visited India for three months

1987

7-27 June, participated in group show *Eye and the Heart: an exhibition of spontaneous work*, Bandon Gallery, Allihies, West Cork

Until 25 November, exhibition of 55 works in acrylic, mixed media, emulsion, collage, watercolour, oil and sand on canvas, board and paper, Tom Caldwell Galleries, 31 Upper Fitzwilliam Street, Dublin 2

September, moved to house at Kilcatherine, Beara Peninsula, West Cork

1988

Converted to Islam in Norwich

1990

Until 7 April, exhibition of 33 acrylics, mixed media works and collages, Tom Caldwell Galleries, 31 Upper Fitzwilliam Street, Dublin 2

16 – 28 July, exhibition staged by Tom Caldwell at Cork Art Society Gallery, 16 Lavitts Quay, Cork

Article on the artist by Rev. Dr. Michael Jackson in *Martello*, spring 1990, pages 11-14

1991

Visited Tunisia for six weeks

From 21 October, *Paintings from the 1980's*, exhibition of 29 oils on canvas and board and one watercolour, Pantheon Gallery, 6 Dawson Street, Dublin

1992

April, visited New York for ten days

From 10 September, exhibition of 30 acrylics and mixed media works, Tom Caldwell Galleries, 31 Upper Fitzwilliam Street, Dublin 2

1993

Visited India for two months

1995

October, *Two and One Exhibition* of 26 works, The Courtyard Gallery, Dublin

1997

Visited Damascus for two months

1999

3-17 November, *Recent Paintings by John Kingerlee*, exhibition of 35 works, Leinster Gallery, Dublin (catalogue introduction by Rev. Dr. Michael Jackson, Dean of Cork)

2000

February, began annual three-monthly visits to Fez, Morocco

2002

From 6 November, *Exhibition of Recent Paintings*, Leinster Gallery, 28 South Frederick Street, Dublin 2

2003

Summer, participated in *Irish Outsider Art*, Crawford Municipal Gallery, Cork, selected by Alannah Hopkin

13-29 November, *An Exhibition of Recent Paintings by John Kingerlee*, Taylor Gallery, Belfast (catalogue foreword by Jonathan Benington)

2004

1 May – 1 July, *The Diversity of John Kingerlee*, exhibition of 35 oils, drawings and mixed media works, Irish Arts Center, New York (catalogue by Jonathan Benington)

From 24 June, *Recent Works on Paper, Dublin, West Cork & Morocco*, Leinster Gallery, 28 South Frederick Street, Dublin 2

Article on the artist by Alannah Hopkin, 'In Search of Authenticity', *Irish Arts Review*, winter 2004, pages 86-91

2005

Buys flat in Granada, with intention of spending five months every year in Spain and Morocco, and the remaining seven months at Kilcatherine

3 – 28 March, *John Kingerlee: Rich in Diversity*, exhibition of 38 oils, acrylics and collages, Vangard Gallery, Cork (catalogue by Rowan Hand and Jonathan Benington)

19 May – 15 June, *John Kingerlee: What Lies Beneath*, exhibition of 32 oils, acrylics and collages, W. J. Morrill Ltd., Dallas, Texas (catalogue by Rowan Hand and Jonathan Benington)

2006

13 February, Works on Paper exhibition opening and Kingerlee book launch by William Zimmer, *New York Times*, Leinster Gallery, Dublin

28 February – 25 March, *John Kingerlee New Paintings*, Anthony Hepworth Fine Art Dealers Ltd., Bath

19 September – 16 October, exhibition of 30 oils, acrylics, collages and mixed media, Galeria Gora, Montreal, Canada